WORD WATCHING

field notes of an amateur philologist

JULIAN BURNSIDE

D0469061

THUNDER'S MOUTH PRESS
NEW YORK

WORD WATCHING
FIELD NOTES OF AN AMATEUR PHILOLOGIST

Published by
Thunder's Mouth Press
An Imprint of Avalon Publishing Group Inc.
245 West 17th Street, 11th Floor
New York, NY 10011

AVALON
publishing group incorporated

Copyright © 2004 by Julian Burnside

First published in Australia by Scribe Publications 2004
First Thunder's Mouth Press edition January 2005

Library of Congress Cataloging-in-Publication Data is available.

ISBN: 1-56025-840-3
ISBN 13: 978-1-56025-840-7

9 8 7 6 5 4 3 2 1

Book design by Miriam Rosenbloom
Printed in the United States of America
Distributed by Publishers Group West

To Kate, who gives my life its meaning

Note

The two great dictionaries of the English language are Samuel Johnson's *Dictionary of the English Language* and the *Oxford English Dictionary*. Throughout this book, I refer to these dictionaries as follows:

> Johnson: Johnson's *Dictionary*, sixth edition, unless otherwise specified
>
> *OED*: *Oxford English Dictionary*
>
> *OED2: Oxford English Dictionary*, second edition

I generally refer to other dictionaries as follows:

> *Bailey*: *Universal Etymological English Dictionary*, by Nathaniel Bailey, 1742
>
> *Webster*: Noah Webster's *American Dictionary of the English Language*, various editions as noted

One other important reference work I refer to frequently is Fowler's *Modern English Usage*, which was published in 1926. A second edition was published in 1968, edited by Sir Ernest Gowers; and a substantially revised edition was published in 1996, edited by Robert Burchfield. Throughout the text, *Fowler* is a reference to the first edition, unless otherwise specified.

Contents

INTRODUCTION

From childhood I found words interesting. I saw the way words engaged people, and I noticed early that using a big word could win the approval of grown-ups. The idea that silence is golden is irrelevant to children under six years of age. It is only imposed long after the child has learned to charm adults with precocious verbal skills.

Words have power, and every child quickly learns that fact.

When I was growing up, we had a copy of *Fowler's Modern English Usage* and a *Shorter Oxford English Dictionary* at home. I was lucky: a less wonderful dictionary would not have had the same impact, and Fowler is not as widely known as he should be. While some aspects of childhood were painful, I always enjoyed browsing in Fowler and 'the dictionary'. Words were a passport to the certainties of adult life, and the dictionary offered the comforting idea of an ordered world. All children crave order amid the uncertainties of childhood.

Fowler was a different matter: here was alphabetical order that did not correspond to any order in the real world. It signified a very quirky view of life indeed. Fowler's articles are given such unpredictable titles that arranging them in alphabetical order was a kind of random trick — they might just as well have been arranged according to their length. Fowler was an uncourtly retired schoolmaster, an atheist who dutifully accompanied his wife to church each Sunday and waited outside until it was time to take her home again. Fowler was full of delightful surprises.

By happy coincidence, *My Fair Lady* appeared on stage and screen during the years when my fascination with language was taking hold. The hero of the piece is Henry Higgins, a philologist who sets out to transport Eliza Doolittle from flower-girl to society debutante by teaching her to speak English 'properly'. *Pygmalion*, the play on which *My Fair Lady* is based, was intended by George Bernard Shaw as a vehicle with which to draw attention to the lamentable state of the English language. His preface to *Pygmalion* contains the following passage:

> The English have no respect for their language, and will not teach their children to speak it. They spell it so abominably that no man can teach himself what it sounds like. It is impossible for an Englishman to open his mouth without making some other Englishman hate or despise him. German and Spanish are accessible to foreigners: English is not accessible even to Englishmen. The reformer England needs today is an energetic phonetic

enthusiast: that is why I have made such a one the hero of a popular play. There have been heroes of that kind crying in the wilderness for many years past.

The character of Henry Higgins was based on Professor Henry Sweet — a late-nineteenth-century English philologist with blunt manners and an abrasive personality. Those deficiencies had taken a gilded Hollywood glow by the time Rex Harrison played the charming, if chauvinistic Henry Higgins in the stage version (1956) and then the film (1964). Rex Harrison's Higgins in the film version reminded me strongly of my absent father. Partly because of that similarity, Higgins became the hero of my youth, and my devotion to language was sealed.

The problem with developing an interest in the workings of the language is that it is hard not to notice the machinery, the stage props, the blunders, and the curiosities. No longer is it possible simply to read or listen: unconsciously, the mind is alert to odd usages, inexplicable idioms, strange connections. This is harmless enough, but inescapable. Soon, even common words provoke further investigation in the dictionary, because every word in the language has a history, and that history passes unnoticed in everyday use. Who would imagine that the word *pedigree* refers to the shape of a crane's foot, or that a *stove* originally referred to a room which was heated, and that it is closely related to *Stube*, the German word for *room*?

Once an interest in language takes hold, the ear becomes tuned to the way words are used. This can be distracting. To hear someone refer to an 'atheist pontificating' immediately conjures up a logical absurdity, since *pontificate* derives from the Latin word for Pope, and means 'to perform the functions of a pontiff or bishop'. How can an atheist pontificate? It jars the ear when a speaker displays their linguistic mastery by referring to a number of *octopi*, since *octopus* comes from Greek (not Latin) and the Greek plural is *octopodes*; but more than this, it is now so thoroughly adopted into English that we should speak of *octopuses*.

oops

The real difficulty is to keep this habit in check. I would not dream of challenging a person who referred to an 'atheist pontificating': the meaning is obvious, and the linguistic slip is unimportant except as a thing of private curiosity. However, there is a great danger that the same bent will lead the afflicted down the dark alley of pedantry, there to lie in wait for the unsuspecting. This is bad. It injures the innocent, and does no service to the language itself: to the contrary, it puts the victim in perpetual fear of the language and its mysteries.

Although Fowler was inclined to be ascerbic, his approach was mostly benign. His article about the great and vexed question of split infinitives begins with an astute observation:

> The English-speaking world may be divided into (1) those who neither know nor care what a split infinitive is; (2) those who do not know but care very much; (3) those who know & condemn; (4) those who know & approve; (5) those who know & distinguish ... those who neither know nor care are the vast majority, & are a happy folk ...

4

Fowler was a realist.

Nevertheless, the habit of noticing how the machinery of language works is a useful one. A well-tuned ear will more quickly spot the occasions, increasingly common, when language is used, not to inform, but to mislead the innocent and unwary. Just as a car enthusiast can quickly detect an odd noise in the motor, likewise the word enthusiast will readily spot evasions, ambiguities, and deceptions.

When a recorded phone message assures us that 'Your call is important to us' it is reasonable to wonder what *important* means, and why phone-answering staff have been 'down-sized', thereby making the message necessary. When a government speaks of 'family values', and locks innocent children behind razor wire, it is useful to examine the true content of its words.

It is easy to forget how powerful words can be. From the ambiguities of the Delphic Oracle to the deceptions of demagogues, we have recognised the need to be alert to false meanings hidden in homely words and deceptive ideas smuggled in disguise as simple truths. Because of this, I am less apologetic than I might otherwise be for allowing a diversion of my childhood to become a distraction in my grown-up life when (it might be said) I should concentrate on more important things.

When truth matters, language is often the first victim; and, in times of stress, truth matters very much.

ALL'S WELL THAT ENDS -*AL*

———◆———

Lots of English words end -*al*. Words of this form generally fall into one of three groups:

- Nouns which become adjectives by adding the adjectival suffix –*al*. This is very common. Some of this first group become nouns again without changing their form.
- Verbs which become nouns by adding the noun suffix –*al*. There are about a dozen common examples of this pattern. Some of these are subsequently pressed into service as adjectives without change of form.
- Words whose form suggests that they follow one or other pattern, but which turn out to be spurious imitators.

The adjectival suffix – *al* generally means *of the kind of*, or *pertaining to*. It reflects the Latin suffix with the same meaning: *-al*, *-alem*. Added to many nouns, it creates a convenient adjective for the associated noun, as for example: *navy—naval*, *norm—normal*; *vestige—vestigial*; *tide—tidal*, etc. There are hundreds of examples of this from *abdominal* to *zonal*. Woody Allen famously lampooned this pattern in his Eggs Benedict sketch, in which he complained of a pain 'in the chestal area'.

A few of the adjectives formed this way become nouns again without further change of form. Sometimes, the fact that the adjective was originally formed from a corresponding noun is obscure or forgotten. Examples of this progression from noun to adjective to noun again are: *commercial*, *confessional*, *periodical*, *journal*, *paralegal*, *terminal*, etc. *Aboriginal* is often enough used in place of *aborigine* to be recognised as a noun, although purists continue to protest; likewise, *oriental* and *continental* for residents of the orient or continental Europe, although these are now disparaged as pejorative. Other, less obvious, examples are *chemical* and, somewhat differently, *pedal*. *Chemic* was another name for an alchemist, but seems to have faded from relevance before even the alchemists themselves. *Pedal* comes from Latin *ped*: foot. *Pedal* was originally an adjective, but is only used as an adjective in the special case of the *pedal pipes* of a pipe organ. They are the pipes activated not from the keyboard — the manuals — but by depressing levers with the feet.

There is a small group of nouns which end *-al* and which result from a parallel use of the suffix. In all its glorious chaos, English can accommodate the use of the suffix not only to convert a noun into an adjective, but also for the quite different task of converting a verb into a noun. There are about a dozen words in ordinary use which follow this pattern. It is uncommon, but easily recognised: *commit–committal*; *dismiss–dismissal*; likewise *arrival*, *approval*, *recital*, *rehearsal*, *survival*, *trial*, and (less obviously) *reprisal* from the archaic meaning of *reprise*: to retake property by force. Fowler (1926) disparages the lazy use of this device to create new nouns where there is an available alternative. His list of bastard nouns formed this way includes *accusal*, *beheadal*, *revisal*, and *refutal*. It is difficult to lament their early demise. But his list also includes *appraisal*, which is now indispensible to the antiques and real estate trades. The Gowers edition of Fowler (1968) raises the white flag by dropping *appraisal* from the list of words to be avoided.

Then come the impostors. *Bridal* and *burial* seem to fit the first and second patterns respectively, but their origins are quite different. *Bridal* was originally *bride-ale*: quite literally the ale drunk at the feast for a newly married bride. It was a noun, not an adjective. Its meaning gradually broadened to embrace the festivities associated with a wedding, and then (as the pattern of the Latin suffix became stronger) it was taken for an adjective. It is not used as a noun any more, although Scott and Tennyson used it as a noun, for archaic effect.

Burial is an Anglo-Saxon word (originally spelt *biriel*, *beryel*, *buriel*, etc). It originally meant *a burying place, grave, or tomb*, and later came to mean the act of burying. It appears to be, but is not, formed on the verb *bury* with the noun suffix. It serves both as a noun–the act or service of interment — and almost as an adjective, in combinations such as burial chamber, burial feast, burial procession.

To these curios can be added *arsenal* (originally — and tortuously — from the Arabic *dar al cina ah*: place of the making); *canal* (reflecting the Latin *canal -em*); *capital* (from the Latin diminutive of head: *capitulum*); *metal* (from Latin *metallum*: a mine); and *pedestal* (from the Italian *piedestallo*: the foot of a stall or shed).

Another example is *admiral* which could, by its form, seem to be related to the verb *admire*. For a short time in the seventeenth century it was in fact used as meaning *admirable*. However, in its normal, naval meaning it derives from the Arabic *amir al bahr*: commander of the sea. The *amir* from which it comes means a commander, and is the same word as *emir*, from which the United Arab Emirates get their name. *Emir* is also a title of honour borne by descendants of Mahommed.

❧

As *bridal* is something of a linguistic imposter, so *bridegroom* conveys a false idea of its true origins. A *groom* is a person who tends to animals, especially horses, by currying and feeding them. It comes from the Anglo-Saxon *grome*: a boy or attendant. The original *bridegroom* was the Anglo-Saxon *brydguma*: that is, a *bride man*. It gradually shifted its form to *brydgome*, and from there the influence of *grome* (attendant) caused a change of form without a concomitant change of meaning. He does not groom the bride: in fact, the Anglo-Saxon tradition forbids him to see her on the wedding day until the wedding ceremony begins and all the grooming has finished.

Another expression which suggests grooming is *curry favour*. The curry-comb is used to groom a horse. The original expression in French was *estriller fauvel*, meaning to curry a fauvel. A *fauvel* was a horse of brownish or reddish yellow. But more than that, it was a specific horse in a twelfth-century French story: a horse which represented fraud and deceit. In the context of the story, the warning not to curry fauvel was advice to avoid wasting care and effort on a deceiver. When the expression came to England, *fauvel* was misunderstood for *favour*, and it was so used by 1500. It is probably for this reason that *currying favour* has a pejorative tinge, although it now speaks poorly of the groom and not the horse. As adopted and varied in English, it makes no literal sense at all, but we understand it because we deem it to mean what it once meant in French.

The Spanish were not seeking to curry favour when they coined the word *flamenco*. The word, which now stands for a proud element of Spanish cultural tradition, was once a disparaging term for natives of Flanders. Those whom we call Flemings the Spanish called *vlamingo* and then *flamenco*.

The Spanish also have the word *batador*: a person who administers a beating, or the instrument used for the purpose. It reflects the pattern of *matador*, *picador*, etc. It is useful for the Spaniards, no doubt, but it has also left a small mark in English. The Spanish *batador* came into English and became *battledore*: a paddle-shaped instrument once used for beating garments during the wash, or flattening them as they pass through the mangle; also the flat-ended instrument for placing loaves in an oven, or taking them out again, and a paddle for a canoe. (Despite the similarity of sound, *paddle* owes nothing to *battledore*).

The game we now call *shuttlecock* was called *battledore and shuttlecock* until the end of the nineteenth century. The *shuttlecock* (or *shuttlecork*) was the piece of cork or other light material with a crown of feathers; the *battledores* were the bats used to hit it across the net. In *Pickwick Papers*, Sam Weller says: 'Battledore and shuttlecock's a wery good game, vhen you an't the shuttlecock and two lawyers the battledores, in which case it gets too excitin' to be pleasant.'

The name of the game has changed, but Weller's sentiment is undimmed in application. Dickens probably did not intend it as a compliment to barristers. He did not like lawyers much, although his son Henry was called to the Bar three years after Dickens died, and later became a leading counsel and was knighted. If coincidence can be permitted to overtake irrelevance, it happens that Sir Henry Dickens once tried a case in front of Hawkins J in which his first witness was a gentleman called Mr Pickwick.

BEASTLY WORDS

◆

The lexicography of animals is rich and fascinating. I have written elsewhere (see 'Collective Nouns') about the various collective expressions used with reference to groups of animals (a murder of crows, a skein of geese, etc). These words are more or less well known, and have a surprisingly long history. They are properly referred to as terms of *venery*. Despite its appearance, *venery* has nothing to do with the goddess of love. It comes from the Latin *venari:* to hunt.

Because venery is the practice or sport of hunting, it is no surprise that *venison* was (originally) any animal normally hunted for meat, or the meat of any animal so caught. So Thoreau in 1884 referred to a hare as a *venison*; and in 1852 a haunch of kangaroo meat was described as venison without any sense of irony.

Hunting is now considered a sport by those who practise it, and deer are much prized by hunters. Hunters express their admiration for the deer by trying to kill it, so most venison nowadays is deer, and the word has narrowed its meaning accordingly.

The young of many species of animals have names which are radically different from the predictable diminutive. Ogden Nash famously wrote:

> Whales have calves,
> Cats have kittens,
> Bears have cubs,
> Bats have bittens,
> Swans have cygnets,
> Seals have puppies,
> But guppies just have little guppies.

The only surprise in his list is *bitten*, which is made up. The list could be supplemented with *heifer*, *poddy*, *fawn*, *foal*, and *joey*. But how many people would immediately remember that a *leveret* is a young hare; or that a baby hog is a *grice* (if still sucking) or a *shoat* (if weaned)? *Pup* is familiar as referring to young dogs and seals, but equally it refers to a young rat or a baby dragon.

While *cygnet* and *gosling* and *squab* are familiar enough, much less so are *eyas* (young hawk) and *poult* (young turkey or domestic chicken). Stranger still are some of the words for young fish of various breeds: young cod are *codling* or *sprag* or *scrod*; baby eels are *elver*; young salmon can also be *sprag*, but in addition they are (in chronological sequence) *parr*, then *smolt* then *grisle* and, at all relevant times, *alevin*. To complete the picture, the spawn of oysters and other bivalves is called *spat*, but this can also be used in reference to bees' eggs — doubtless a frequent source of confusion.

Everyone knows what *bovine*, *feline*, and *canine* mean. Less familiar are the adjectives associated with some other animals: *dasypodid* (pertaining to armadillos); *vespertilian* (bats); *vituline* (calves); *pithecoid* and *simian* (monkeys); and *pongid* (gorillas and orang-utans).

The albatross holds an honoured place in the folklore of the sea. It produced grief and guilt for the sailor who shot one, and lived to tell the tale to the wedding guests in Coleridge's *The Rime of the Ancient Mariner*:

> And the good south wind still blew behind,
> But no sweet bird did follow,
> Nor any day for food or play
> Came to the mariners' hollo!
>
> And I had done an hellish thing,
> And it would work 'em woe:
> For all averred, I had killed the bird
> That made the breeze to blow.
> Ah wretch! said they, the bird to slay,
> That made the breeze to blow!

The Rime of the Ancient Mariner was written in 1798. Less than 100 years earlier, William Dampier had written of a bird called the *algatross*; not long before that, sailors called it the *alcatras*. This was at a time when English sailors rarely saw one. They had the word from Dutch and Portuguese sailors who, as it happens, were talking about a different bird altogether.

The albatross is a petrel, a member of the order *Diomedea*, which is seen in the southern oceans, and so was beyond the range of most English sailors before the seventeenth century. The *alcatras* is what we now know as the pelican (genus *Pelecanus*). The pelican's original Portugese name — *al-catras* — is the scoop or bucket (*catras*) on a water-wheel. It comes originally from the Arab water-lifting device *al quadus*. The Arabs named the pelican by a related metaphor — *al sagga*: the water-carrier.

The notorious US prison in San Francisco Bay, Alcatraz, was named after the island on which it stands. A Spanish lieutenant, Juan Manuel de Ayala, explored it in 1755, and named it *Isla de los Alcatraces*, after the large pelican population there.

⌘

Thomas Hobbes popularised Leviathan in his book of the same name, published in 1651. In chapter 28 he wrote:

> Hitherto I have set forth the nature of man, whose pride and other passions have compelled him to submit himself to government; together with the great power of his governor, whom I compared to LEVIATHAN, taking that comparison out of the two last verses of the one-and-fortieth of Job; where God, having set forth the great power of Leviathan, calleth him king of the proud. 'There is nothing,' saith he, 'on earth to be compared with him. He is made so as not to be afraid.

There is great conjecture about what this beast was, on which Hobbes' metaphor was built. The Leviathan is mentioned four times in the King James version of the Bible. The references in Job 41:1, in Psalms 74:14, and in Psalms 104:26 are consistent with Leviathan being a whale.

All references to the Leviathan give the sense that it was a huge beast. The reference in Psalms 104 suggests a whale. Milton, in *Paradise Lost* (vii, 412), calls it the 'hugest of living creatures' — which the whale is. Herman Melville, at the start of *Moby Dick*, takes pains to claim the credit for whales as the Leviathan, but his agenda was clear. Anatole France was equally confident. In *Penguin Island* (1908) he says:

And Leviathan passed by hurling a column of water up to the clouds.

However, in Isaiah 27:1 the following appears:

In that day the Lord with his sore and great and strong sword shall punish leviathan the piercing serpent, even leviathan that crooked serpent; and he shall slay the dragon that [is] in the sea.

Johnson acknowledged the uncertainty, and defined Leviathan as:

A water animal mentioned in the book of Job. By some imagined the crocodile, but in poetry generally taken for the whale.

Only a poet could confuse the whale with a serpent, or with a reptile of any sort. The passage from Isaiah cannot be referring to a whale: the reference to 'a crooked serpent' and 'that dragon … in the sea' suggests a crocodile, or else a wholly mythical creature.

The possibility that Leviathan is a creature of the imagination gains support from Babylonian literature, which records a battle between the god Marduk and the multi-headed serpent-dragon Tiamat. This story prefigures St George and the dragon. A parallel story in Canaanite writing has Baal fighting Leviathan at Ugarit in Northern Syria: a story more consistent with Leviathan being a huge crocodile, or a dragon.

A creature which is, by definition, imaginary is the *chimera*. Its name comes from the Greek for he-goat. It is a fire-breathing monster with a lion's head, a goat's body, and a serpent's tail. Other accounts rearrange the body parts, which is both possible and painless in imaginary beasts. *Chimera* now is used almost exclusively to refer to a 'wild fancy or unfounded conception'.

Since Hobbes dressed Leviathan in the raiment of government, and Freud lured dragons to the analyst's couch, such beasts have faded from popular imagination. They are all chimeras now.

The platypus should be chimerical: its oddities are nicely captured by Ogden Nash:

I like the duck-billed platypus
Because it is anomalous

Word Watching

I like the way it raises its family —
Partly birdly, partly mammaly
I like its independent attitude:
Let no-one call it a duck-billed platitude.

BLACK HOLES

—◆—

It is a curious thing about the English language, that although it has a vast vocabulary and rich idiomatic variations, it lacks words for some common and useful ideas. This is so, despite the fact that we have words for ideas so obscure that they can hardly expect to be used more than once in a lifetime. For example:

abaciscus: a square compartment enclosing a part or the entire pattern or design of a Mosaic pavement

catapan: the officer who governed Calabria and Apulia under the Byzantine emperors

denariate: a portion of land worth a penny a year

holluschickie: young males of the northern, Pribilof, or Alaska fur seal

pitarah: a basket or box used in travelling by palankeen to carry the traveller's clothes

spetch: a piece or strip of undressed leather, a trimming of

hide, used in making glue or size
wennish: of the nature of a wen
turdiform: having the form or appearance of a thrush

Philip Howard — sometime literary editor of *The Times*, and a splendid writer about words — calls these gaps 'black holes'. In deference to him, I adopt the same tag although it is inappropriate. The intended meaning is a gap, or an absence where a presence might be expected. By contrast, a black hole is caused by the presence of an enormous mass concentrated to an extent inconceivable to all but physicists. The gravitational pull of this mass is so great that nothing — not even light — can escape from it, once the gravitational horizon has been crossed. We misuse *black hole* colloquially just as we misuse *quantum leap* (see 'Change #2'), but only physicists are likely to be upset or confused.

Philip Howard identifies *Schadenfreude* as one of the black holes in English. One commentator (R.C. Trench) celebrates this gap, saying:

> What a fearful thing is it that any language should have a word expressive of the pleasure which men feel at the calamities of others; *for the existence of the word bears testimony to the existence of the thing*. And yet in more than one, such a word is found: in the Greek *epikairekakia*, in the German, *Schadenfreude*.

It is rare to see such refinement of feeling deployed in the service of philology, but relations between the English and the Germans have always been complex. Personally, I think *Schadenfreude* is a useful and expressive word, and much to be preferred to *epikairekakia*.

Terry Lane has defined *Schadenfreude* as the sensation experienced when you see two Mercedes Benz collide: but that may reflect his preference for Australian-made cars more than his proud egalitarianism. In either case, it is a near-perfect definition for a sentiment which dares not speak its name in English. Clive James admits to *Schadenfreude* when he sees his rival's book in the remainders bin.

Trench's point is neatly made in the Victorian laws against homosexuality. Since Queen Victoria refused to accept the possibility of homosexual attraction between women, the offence created by parliament was confined in application to men (as Oscar Wilde soon found to his grief). The island of Lesbos, where Sappho had made her home, suggested the adjective *lesbian*, which had for a long time been used neutrally to refer to inhabitants of the island. In 1890 Billings used it as an adjective to refer to female homosexual love. While Billings is given by *OED2* as the first use in this meaning, Diarmid MacCulloch in his *Reformation* (Penguin 2003) writes that the word was used in this sense already in the eighteenth century. In 1925 Aldous Huxley first used *lesbian* as a noun.

The presence in English of an un-naturalised foreign word is a fair indicator of a black hole in the language. The presence of a convenient foreign word very likely prevents the emergence of an English equivalent. So, expressions such as *savoir faire*, *déjà vu*, *décolletage*, *faux pas*, *outré*, *de trop*, and *l'esprit d'escalier* are well-understood and very useful. They serve a purpose which is not adequately served by existing English words.

However, although these and similar expressions fill a gap, they leave unfilled room around the edges. English is very ready to create variants of existing words, in order to allow (for example) a noun to generate a verb, an adjective, and an adverb. Thus the language can be used more flexibly to deploy the central idea. *Grovelling*, for example, is an adverb, not a participle. But it looks like a participle, so we freely backform a verb *to grovel*, and a noun *a grovel*. A vast number of English words have identical or similar relatives which serve as other grammatical forms.

By contrast, un-naturalised foreign words and phrases do not lend themselves to conversion into related grammatical forms. So, *déjà vu* is a useful noun, but how to make an adjective which describes an occurrence which has the characteristics of *déjà vu*? Likewise, you could not possibly say a person smiled *Schadenfreudishly*, as their enemy *faux pas*ed their way through a conversation.

Although *savoir faire* is a pair of verbs in French, it can only be used as a noun in English. Such a pity it cannot be used adjectivally: *she was as savoir faire as he was gauche*. By contrast, *gauche* has been naturalised: we speak more readily of *gaucheness* than the correct *gaucherie*. *Naïve* has also been naturalised: at least in part. It can be used as an adjective, and becomes *naïvely* when an adverb is needed. Nevertheless the accepted noun for it is *naiveté* (French) rather than *naiveness* or *naivity*.

Argument by *reductio ad absurdum* is useful and common, especially in the realms of philosophical and legal discourse. Obviously, it cannot be converted into a different grammatical form. In order to describe the mode of argument, we say it is an *argument by reductio ad absurdum*. Happily, there is an adjective-adverb pair with the same meaning: *apagogical*, *apagogically*.

Unhappily, there is no equivalent way of expressing the adverbial phrase *mutatis mutandis* in adjectival form or as a verb (*mutatis mutandis* is frequently used by lawyers. It means 'things being changed that have to be changed' — that is, making alterations necessary to allow equivalent cases to be compared). How handy it would be to ask a typist to *mutandise* a summons into a draft order, or to *mutatise* a set of interrogatories into a form appropriate to the facts of the next case. *Mutate* would be good, but it is taken already for a different meaning.

It is probably a good working test of naturalisation of a foreign word that it can be converted into other grammatical forms. It is one of the great strengths of the English language that it absorbs so many foreign words and then treats them as native. In *Modern English Usage* (1926), H.W. Fowler lists a number of French words and phrases, with guidance for their pronunciation and plural forms. They are listed, clearly, as un-naturalised foreign words. It is instructive to see that the list includes many words which are still obviously foreign (*chic, en famille, metayage, petit, pis aller, sang froid, soi-disant*), but it also includes many which have since been naturalised: *ballet, bureau, calorie, carafe, casserole, chassis, clairvoyant, diplomat, gauche, insouciant, liaison, macabre, massage, mayonnaise, nuance, panache, provenance, reduction, regime, restaurant, ricochet, sabotage*, and *verve*.

Despite all this wanton borrowing from other languages, there remain obvious gaps in English. We need an equivalent to the Italian *magari*, which translates roughly as 'Ah but that it were so'. We have *if only*, and *you wish*, but neither quite captures it.

Why do we not have a word for the sensation of disaster narrowly averted and later remembered from the vantage point of safety? It is different from fear: that was the sensation at the time the danger was present, and the outcome was unknown. Later, usually in the dark, unsleeping hours before dawn, the sense of what might have been returns with added elements of guilt, shame and sweating relief, in a mixture which is too powerful and familiar to be un-named.

And what of its approximate opposite: the instantaneous sensation when, for example, you are pulled over by a booze bus, and have not had a drink for two weeks! Despite demonstrable innocence, there is a flash of guilt — *empty guilt* perhaps? — which, I suspect, most people experience.

We should have a word to take the place of *yes*, when it is used in conversation to signify that the hearer understands, but does not agree with, the argument being developed by the speaker. It is possible to use the phrase *I hear what you say*, but this has a dismissive connotation which makes it dangerous at times. I understand that judges find it particularly irritating when used by counsel; and on the few occasions I have seen my opponent use it in argument, the effect has invariably helped my case.

And whilst I am advocating linguistic inventions, can we have a word for the sensation when sleepiness swerves briefly back into alertness at the moment your head drops forward during a dull lecture, for example. One writer has suggested *whipnap*, which is perfect and should be adopted.

We need a noun cognate with *ignore*, but different from *ignorance*. 'She treated him with contempt and ignore' catches a meaning we all need to express, but *ignore* cannot be used this way except for humourous effect. *Ignoral* is sometimes seen, but is also jocular. *Ignoration* has this sense as a secondary meaning, which is recorded as last used in 1881. Perhaps we should revive it.

BUSHRANGERS

———◆———

In the second edition of the *Oxford English Dictionary* (*OED2*), Rolf Boldrewood is quoted 184 times in illustration of about 160 words. Appropriately so. Boldrewood (Thomas Alexander Browne, 1826–1915) was the first Australian author to capture faithfully the emerging Australian variant of the English language. Although born in London, he came to Australia as a child and spent the rest of his life here. He ran a farm in Victoria, and was later a police magistrate and a goldfields commissioner in the Victorian and New South Wales goldfields. He had a good ear for idiom and had the courage to write it down faithfully. His characters are the first in Australian literature to speak real Australian with no sense of parody.

Boldrewood did for the Australian language what Tom Roberts did for the Australian landscape: he removed the European filter and saw Australia through Australian eyes. Boldrewood's *Robbery Under Arms* is a comprehensive glossary of the language of bushrangers, and Dick Marston is the first truly Australian character in our literature.

When Ned Kelly ambushed the police at Stringybark Creek he called, 'Bail up. Put up your hands'. Much later, after his arrest, Kelly was asked by Constable McIntyre why he had ambushed the police party. He responded, 'If we had not done so, you would have found us and shot us. We had bad horses and no money and simply wanted to make a rise.'

Bail up and *make a rise* are early Australian colloquialisms. *Make a rise* is not used at all currently. *Bail up* is rarely heard, although you might occasionally hear of a person being *bailed up* in some awkward spot.

Surprisingly, *bail up* comes originally from dairy farming and was adopted *ad hoc* by bushrangers. From the early days of white settlement in Australia, the frame designed for holding a cow's head steady during milking was called the *bail* (also spelled *bale*). The farmer wanting to get his cows co-operating would shout 'Bail up' as he pushed them into the bails. According to *OED2*, this usage is specific to Australia and New Zealand. However, Morris' *Dictionary of Austral English* (1898) notes that this usage was also found in Ireland, and in the dialect of five English counties. In any event, the idiom was recorded in Australia as early as 1846. No doubt it had been in spoken use well before that.

By the time Ned Kelly told Lonigan and McIntyre to *bail up*, the expression had been current for several generations. As Sidney J. Baker has noted (*The Australian Language*, 1945), the cry of *bail up*, in the general sense of demanding submission to the speaker's will, would have come readily to the tongue of that group for whom bushranging was a realistic career option. And so it did. From 1840 to the end of the century, *bail up* was commonly used in the way Ned Kelly used it. One of the illustrative quotations in *OED2* is from Kelly himself.

It is clear from the various recorded uses of *bail up* that its central meaning involves submission to the speaker's will. For example, the quotation from Nisbett's *Bush Girl's Romance* (1894) reads: 'Reginald … acted like a wise man and "bailed up", that is, he dropped his knife and threw up his hands as a sign of submission'.

The first edition of the *OED* doubted whether the bushranger's use of *bail up* owed anything at all to the dairy farmer's expression. The question seems to have been answered authoritatively by Rolf Boldrewood in *Robbery Under Arms*, published in book form in 1888. In chapter 47 he writes:

> The same talk for cows and Christians! That's how things get stuck in the talk in a new country. Some old hand like father, as had spent all his mornings in the cowyard, had taken to the bush and tried his hand at sticking up people. When they came near enough … he'd pop out … with his musket (and say) 'Bail up, d___ you'.

Given the etymological observation implicit in the passage above, it is surprising that the *OED2* does not cite Boldrewood for the meaning of *bail up*.

In the famous Jerilderie letter, dictated by Ned Kelly but

written by Joe Byrne in early 1879, Kelly criticises many aspects of the colonial police force:

> a parcel of big ugly fat-necked wombat headed big bellied
> magpie legged narrow hipped splay-footed sons of Irish
> Bailiffs or English landlords which is better known as …
> the Victoria Police …

He discusses the idea that police witnesses regularly perjure themselves and adds that 'it was by that means and by hiring cads they get promoted'. This use of *cad* is puzzling. According to *OED2*, *cad* means: 'An assistant or confederate of a lower grade, as a bricklayer's labourer (dial.); a familiar, chum'.

Neither of these meanings makes much sense in the context of the Jerilderie letter. The second seems an unlikely usage for Kelly.

Another obscure meaning of *cad*, specifically from Ireland, is a *cade lamb*; that is, a tame or pet lamb. This makes sense in context, but only just.

But there is another possibility. *Cad* was Australian slang for a cicada, now out of use. It seems likely that the reference was to police informers who, like a cicada, will make a lot of noise when prompted. For some odd reason, we have developed (and since forgotten) a lot of slang terms for cicadas: *baker*, *floury baker*, *floury miller*, *cad*, *green Monday*, *yellow Monday*, *miller*, *mealyback*, *red eye*, and *double drummer*. I confess that, apart from the last, these make no sense to me at all. Clearly there is something about cicadas I have missed.

Kelly's other interesting colloquialism, *make a rise*, sounds suitably revolutionary. It is clear enough that *rise* has, as one meaning, *uprising*. While it is true that Kelly has had attributed to him revolutionary tendencies (tendencies recently recast as republican), it seems very unlikely that his comment to Constable McIntyre was meant as an admission of a revolutionary purpose. Apart from anything else, he was too astute to inflame a difficult situation by adding armed revolt to the catalogue of his crimes.

Make a rise means to *strike gold*, and is so used by Boldrewood in *The Miner's Right* (1890) and later by Ion Idriess in *Lightning Ridge* (1940). In the more general sense of striking sudden good luck, it was used by W.T. Porter in *Quarter Race in Kentucky* (1836), where the luck came in the form of a gambling game that rejoiced in the improbable name *chuck a luck*.

At his fortified compound in the Wombat Ranges, Ned Kelly had been working for gold, as well as stealing horses, and growing corn for whisky. Gold mining was still a boom industry in Victoria in 1878, and fortunes were still being made. It was the one activity which offered the prospect of riches for the unskilled and unemployed. It is overwhelmingly likely that Kelly's comment to McIntyre was an unselfconscious declaration that he was trying to make an honest living. One hundred and twenty years later, the idiom has lost its innocent meaning and appears, mistakenly, to carry a sinister threat.

CACOPHEMIOUS

◆

In 1995 the Victorian Bar's weekly news sheet, *In Brief*, carried a raging debate about the word *cacophemious*. I was content to be a silent spectator until the anonymous editor declared the poll, and in so doing compounded and concealed his/her original error. Even this circumstance might not have moved me to thumbnail and tar, but the whole episode is a good demonstration of a common mechanism by which language evolves.

Issue No. 54 of *In Brief* (21 February 1995) introduced a new column titled 'Briefly: Compliments, Complaints and Cacophemism'. It was to be a form for readers' letters 'of 50 words or less'. That limitation was flagrantly ignored by Habersberger, QC (as he then was) in Issue No. 55, and again by Nicholson CJ and Lord Nicholls in Issue No. 56. Power chatters, and endless power chatters endlessly.

The true polemical style of the column got going with the help of Jessup, QC on 4 April (Issue No. 57). He said he did not want to sound *cacophemious*, but questioned the new cheap-photocopy look of the Bar's own Thunderer. The editor attempted to stir debate on this fascinating question, but got instead a debate about the existence, etymology, and meaning of *cacophemious*.

Carolyn Sparke (No. 58, 24 April) asserted (correctly) that the word had not (yet) found a home in any serious dictionary. Ross and Giudice (No. 59, 9 May) dressed it up with spurious etymologies, and attributed a meaning to it accordingly. The editor thereupon declared Ross and Guidice right, and Sparke wrong: a cowardly escape from his/her original solecism.

Cacophemy and, by extension *cacophemious* (and, while we are at it, what about *cacophemity* and *cacophemeral?*), is an error for *cacophony*, presumably modelled on the example of *euphony–euphemy–euphemism*. Because its root is familiar, and its erroneous form follows a familiar example, the intended meaning is tolerably clear.

Guidice made the point that it was a quibble that the word was not in the dictionary. That is the end-point of Lewis Carroll's Humpty Dumpty principle: words mean what I say they mean, nothing more and nothing less. The fact remains that the coin is newly minted, and nonetheless counterfeit for having passed into circulation at full value.

The process is as old as language itself. English has many words, now eminently respectable, which are originally corrupt or erroneous forms of 'real' words. For example:

avoirdupois: properly averdepois
compost: compot
curfew: couvrefeu
filibuster: free booter
sciatic: ischiatic
lingo: lingua
scruff: of neck, scuff of neck
syllabus: sittubas
talisman: tailasan
alligator: al lagarto
apron: naperon
bandicoot: pandi-kokku
banister: baluster
denim: de Nimes
cartridge: cartouche

The process occurs in at least two ways.

First, with commonly used words which are difficult to say, the pronunciation rapidly erodes, and the commonly accepted form is thereby altered (*hautbois* became *hoboy* then *oboe*; *peruke* became *periwig* then *wig*).

Second, words used only rarely are inaccurately recalled, but are understood by virtue of their similarity to the true word, and the context in which they are used (*cacophony* becomes *cacophemy* and thence *cacophemism, cacophemious,* and so on).

Oddly, the process sometimes reverses itself. In the seventeeth century, *asparagus* became *sparagrass* then *sparrow-grass*. In 1791, Walker's *Pronouncing Dictionary* said: "'Sparrow-grass' is so general that "asparagus" has an air of stiffness and pedantry'. The wheel turned full circle in the mid-nineteenth century: *asparagus* 'returned into literary and for like use, leaving *sparrow-grass* to the illiterate …' (*OED2*).

Another example of the process is *curare*. Originally, it was *wurari* or *wurali*. As is well-known, it is a poison formerly used by South American indians on their arrow tips. Its botanical name is *strychnos toxifera*. Well named, because the Greek *toxos* is an archer's bow; *toxophily* is a love of archery. A *poison arrow* might be considered a tautology.

⁂

The English language develops by many mechanisms. Two of the most fruitful are the mechanisms of back-formation and parallel construction. *Cacophemious*, if treated as an utterance in English rather than classical Greek, appears to be an instance of parallel construction.

There are many instances of parallel construction. Many start life as a conscious attempt at humour, and gradually mature into general acceptance. So, from the original *Marathon* (named after the place where one victorious Athenian started his long homeward run with the good news of victory), we get the obvious *marathon* for a race over the same distance; thence *jogathon*, *talkathon*, *phonathon*, and so-athon. Similarly, from *alcohol* (an Arab word, *al koh'l*, the name for *corrylium*, a fine powder for colouring the eyelids) comes *alcoholic*; and from that *chocaholic*, *workaholic*, *spendaholic*, and *computerholic*. From the Russian *sputnik* we have *beatnik*, *peacenik*, *nogoodnik*, *straightnik*, *kibbutznik*. However, each of these seems to be fading as the 1950s recede from cultural memory.

Generally, the process happens because an affix is recognised but not fully understood for its original meaning. A fruitful prefix to have undergone this transformation is *mini-*. It came into vogue in the 1960s when British Leyland released its hugely successful Mini Minor. It is a reminder of the linguistic novelty of the name at the time, that the car was initially released in Australia as the Morris 850: *Mini Minor* was thought a bit racy for delicate Australian linguistic tastes. But it soon became celebrated world-wide as the Mini Minor, and was followed by a flood of *mini-* words which has not since abated: *mini-cab, mini-cam, mini-coat, mini-computer, mini-skirt*, and even *mini-marathon*. There are very few noun compounds which cannot accept *mini-* as a prefix and be readily understood.

It is interesting (but irrelevant) that *mini-* derives from a misunderstanding, and that the original use of *mini-* was as much of a parallel construction as its followers. The word which inspired *Mini Minor* was *miniature*. Everyone understands *miniature* in its main current signification as *a reduced image or representation*. It was not always so. In the days before the moveable-type printing press made written material widely accessible, books were written and illustrated by hand. Each book was intrinsically valuable, because of the amount of time necessarily spent on its creation. Pious monks spent their lives transcribing important texts. Not surprisingly, they included some elaborate flourishes: initial letters were often highly elaborate, and red-lead was used to add highlights and decorative illustrations. Although the practice was known in Egyptian times, it is first seen in Greek and Roman texts in the fourth century AD, and in Byzantium in the fifth century. Until the seventh century in Byzantium, the style was relatively restrained, but the art blossomed from the seventh to the sixteenth century, by which time it had become a self-conscious indulgence, in view of the spread of the printing press.

The style of illumination of manuscripts became increasingly elaborate and, by the seventh century, other colours were being used to supplement red. But red-lead was the original and dominant pigment. The Latin word for red-lead was *minium.* The process of using it in illuminations was called *miniating*, and the product was *miniature.* Thus the first definition given to *miniature* by *OED2* is 'The action or process of rubricating letters or of illuminating a manuscript'.

Since Latin has *minimus* and *minor,* both with meanings associated with smallness, it is not surprising that *miniature* came to have its current dominant meaning.

Back-formation is likewise a fruitful source of new words. It has a lot in common with parallel construction, since each depends on the mind's instinctive recognition of patterns in word structures. A back-formation is the creation of a new word from an existing word, on the pattern of existing pairs of words which show the same pattern of construction. In 1791 there existed *creditor* and *credit. Editor* existed, and Enfield assumed or invented *edit.* There is an astounding number of back-formed words in the language (including *back-formed*). Here are a few examples, with the dates on which the back-formation is first recorded:

suckling >> suckle (1408)
grovelling >> grovel (1593)
sightseeing >> sightsee (1960)
cobbler >> cobble (1496)
hawker >> hawk (1542)
part taker >> partake (1561)
eavesdropper >> eavesdrop (1606)
burglar >> burgle (1870)
sculptor >> sculpt (1934)
procession >> process (1814)
intuition >> intuit (1840)
electrocution >> electrocute (1889)
automation >> automate (1950)
television >> televise (1950)

The *OED2* identifies 947 words as back-formations, from *ablate* (back-formed from *ablation*, 1542) to *york* (back-formed from *yorker*, 1882).

The process is an endless source of new words for the language, available as need arises. On first hearing a new-coined word, various people react differently (unless they react indifferently). The English-speaking world might be divided into those who rail against these processes of language change; those who do not notice or care (the largest group); and those who care but discriminate. Not all members of the last group, in which I would claim a place, would apply the same criteria for distinguishing those changes which are to be welcomed from those which are to be resisted as barbarisms.

Let me suggest a few criteria to test the legitimacy of a new word or usage.

Does it duplicate an already existing word or usage, or does it fill a gap? Is it elegant or clumsy? Is it coined consciously, or by mistake for an existing word with the same meaning? Is it a useful extension to the language, or an expedient to help the writer finish a badly constructed sentence? And, most importantly, does its use serve to aid comprehension, or to confuse the writer's meaning?

CHANGE #1

The process of change in language includes the drift of meaning, the invention of new words, and the obsolescence of existing words. It is interesting to survey a list of words once disparaged by the arbiters of language as not proper English words. In 1818, Dr Todd published a revised edition of Johnson's *Dictionary*, the first edition not supervised by Johnson himself. It draws on an annotated folio edition which had been owned by Horne Tooke, the politician and pamphleteer. Tooke had compiled a list of words found in Johnson's *Dictionary* which he regarded as 'false English'. This list is reproduced in the Todd edition. It includes such curiosities as *abditive*, *acatalectic*, *conjobble*, *dorture*, and *warhable*.

However, it also includes *justiciable*, *fragile*, *mandible*, *mobile*, *cognitive*, and *horticulture*. How the fortunes of words can vary.

Most of the words that perish disappear, leaving no trace

except in the dictionaries. Some others leave a reminder of their former existence, in a variant modified by a prefix or a suffix. *Gruesome*, *noisome*, and *cumbersome* are all in daily use. Oddly enough, *grue*, *noy*, and *cumber* all existed once but have fallen from use. To *grue* is to feel terror or horror, to shudder, tremble, or quake. To *cumber* is to overwhelm or rout; also to harass, distress, or trouble. To *noy* is to trouble, vex, or harass; it is an aphetic form of *annoy*.

Uncouth occasionally gives rise to the jocular *couth*. In fact, *couth* exists with the meaning you would suppose. It survives in Scottish dialect as *couthie*. It is derived from the German *kennen*: to know, which also survives in English ('beyond our ken') and dialectical Scottish ('do ye ken John Peel').

P.G. Wodehouse used *gruntled* as a humorous opposite of *disgruntled*. *Gruntle* came first. It means *to utter little grunts*. As a noun, it is the contented grunting sound made by happy pigs; it is also a pig's snout. A pig whose nose is actually or metaphorically out of joint is aptly described as *disgruntled*.

Why did we let *inkle* slip into oblivion? Its relative, *inkling*, still flourishes in idiom. *To inkle* is to communicate in an undertone or whisper, to give a hint of something. A perfect word and a useful purpose — it ought to be revived.

On the other hand, *incipient* is not the negative of anything; it comes directly from the Latin *incipere*, which means *to begin*. Likewise *inchoate*, which comes from the Latin *inchoare*, which also means *to begin*.

In an English case decided in 1951, a judge said '... until that consent was given, the contract was wholly ineffective ... It only became cohate on September 25 ...' This solecism is exposed by Megarry in *Miscellany at Law* at page 33, and the treatment is expanded and the scorn redoubled in *A Second Miscellany at Law* at pages 160–61. It is ironic, then, that the correct form of the original Latin is *incohare*, so *cohate* at least shows an intuitive grasp of a hidden truth, even though it is wrong on other grounds.

Another curious victim of the process of change is *whelm*. The *OED2* records that some — but not all — of its senses are obsolete. Those which, at least according to the dictionary, are in theory still current include:

> to throw (something) over violently or in a heap upon something else so as to cover or crush or smother it

and

> to cover completely with water or other fluid so as to ruin or destroy, to destroy or submerge

The second sense makes *overwhelm* seem tautologous. *Underwhelm*, though entertaining, is plainly wrong.

CHANGE #2

———◆———

The world of language is littered with durable solecisms which eventually come to be accepted in their 'false' meanings through consistent use. In other essays (see 'Collective Nouns' and 'Mistaken Meanings') I discuss *fulsome*, *ilk*, *helpmeet*, *syllabus*, and others as words whose current meaning, once considered erroneous, is now entrenched.

The language of science is a steady source of words which suffer this fate. However, the process of derailing the true meaning of scientific words is usually swift. If the original meaning of ordinary words suffers the death of a thousand cuts, victims from the lexicon of science are put to the sword as soon as they appear in a popular newspaper. The reason is not hard to find: journalists like strange, evocative words to add rouge to the cheeks of indifferent writing; and the reading public does not, as a rule, understand more about science than survived reluctant Thursdays in the high school science laboratory.

Consider the fate of *quantum leap*. In popular usage, it means 'a sudden, very large change in amount, position or attitude'. Its true meaning is almost the opposite. Quantum mechanics was the creation — perhaps 'discovery' is more accurate — of Max Planck. He announced his theory at a meeting of the German Physical Society in Berlin on 14 December 1900. He postulated that energy exists only in discrete packets, or quanta, which were irreducible and indivisible. From that proposition he explained the wave-particle duality of electro-magnetic waves which had puzzled scientists for a long time: light and other forms of electro-magnetic energy exhibit properties associated with waves, but they also exhibit properties associated with particles. How could such inconsistent properties co-exist in electro-magnetic energy? Quantum mechanics provided the answer.

Planck postulated that electrons could only move in particular orbits and, while they might move from one orbit to another, they could not move to a new orbit lying between the fixed orbits. To move between orbits involved receiving, or losing, a quantum of energy. The quantum was indivisible, hence the impossibility of intermediate orbits. The jump from one orbit to another was associated with the gain or loss of a quantum of energy, so it was a quantum jump. It is the *smallest* change in position possible in the known universe or, for that matter, the unknown universe, given the overwhelming evidence that quantum mechanics accurately describes the physics of all sub-atomic particles.

Quantum mechanics developed over the course of the next 30 years, baffling everyone. Like most scientific revolutions, it caught the imagination of the press, and the *quantum jump* (soon the *quantum leap*) was picked up as a vogue expression. Perhaps because the theory itself was so revolutionary and its effects so profound, its central concept, the quantum jump, almost instantaneously came to be used as signifying a gigantic step.

In a very different way, the prefix *cyber* has belatedly been picked up by internet enthusiasts, and is now loosely associated with the worldwide web. *Cyber* derives originally from the Greek *kubernetos*, meaning steersman. In its first adoption into English, it appeared as *gubernate* (1432), *gubern* (govern, 1520) *gubernator* (governor, ruler, 1522), and cognate expressions such as *gubernacle*, *gubernacular*, *gubernance*, and so on. In the USA it is in common use as *gubernatorial* (USA, 1734), because the state governors are elected, and an adjective is needed to describe the elections.

Apart from the American usage, the word is confined to the dusty corners of language. But in 1948, Norbert Wiener wrote a seminal work on communication theory and control systems, entitled *Cybernetics*, in which he said: 'We have decided to call the entire field of control and communication theory, whether in the machine or in the animal, by the name Cybernetics.'

In its most popular manifestation, cybernetics is characterised by the use of information feed-back as an integral component of a control mechanism. Thus, the thermostat in an air-conditioning system detects the temperature of the room and feeds that information back to the heating unit; the heating unit produces more or less heat;

the temperature changes; the thermostat detects the change in temperature and feeds the information back to the heating unit; and so the feed-back loop continues. That is cybernetics in action.

For reasons which are entirely obscure, people who spend a lot of time surfing the internet are now called *cybernauts*; the virtual space they create and populate is called *cyberspace*; anyone with a regulatory role or minatory attitude on the net is likely to be referred to as a *cybercop*; the collection of text information on the net is a *cyberlibrary*; the fact that pornographic material is to be found in the cyberlibrary has produced the term *cybersex*; good web graphics are *cyberart*. In short, if you want to sound like an old hand on the internet, just add *cyber-* to any word which is capable of taking a prefix.

The unifying sense in which the prefix is used is 'of or pertaining to the internet'. It is difficult to see how the usage arose. There is no apparent connection between cybernetics and the internet: on the contrary, the internet is the largest uncontrolled information system the world has ever seen.

And finally, a *parting shot*. It is not really erroneous since its literal meaning is accurately caught in its common usage. As the *OED2* says, it has been in use in one form or another since the sixteenth century:

'Thus much I must say for a parting blow.'
(Robert Greene, 1592)

'With this parting shot, Nancy flung into the house.'
(Hall Caine, 1894)

But it derives from an earlier, metaphorical, expression and has replaced it because of their phonological similarity. The original expression is *Parthian shot*. By about 170 BC the Parthian region was independent of the Seleucid kingdom, and in 55 BC the ineffectual Roman general Crassus was defeated by the Parthians, who used a home-grown tactic to great effect. The Parthian horsemen would ride towards their enemy and let fly a volley of arrows, then turn in retreat. Thinking the Parthians' resources exhausted, the Romans would follow the retreating horsemen. But, great horsemen that they were, the Parthians would rise in their saddles and, turning, fire another volley into the unsuspecting Romans. Thus the devastating final shot in apparent or actual retreat became known as the Parthian shot. Here lies the subtle distinction between the two expressions: a parting shot is one necessarily associated with departure; a Parthian shot may be the purpose of a feigned withdrawal.

> 'Poison,' said Sherlock Holmes curtly, and strode off. 'One other thing, Lestrade,' he added, turning round at the door: "Rache" is the German for revenge; so don't lose your time looking for Miss Rachel.' With which Parthian shot he walked away, leaving the two rivals open mouthed behind him.' (*A Study in Scarlet*, Conan Doyle)

Tom Stoppard caught something of the original, while using the modern variation: 'He smiles briefly at them without mirth, and starts to back out, his parting shot rising again.' (*Rosencrantz & Guildenstern are Dead* ii. 57)

CHANGE #3

In other essays, I discuss words whose meanings have drifted over generations of use. However, many words which still bear their original meaning take a form which has drifted from the original — generally due to the difficulty of pronunciation coupled with frequent use, or confusion of an unfamiliar term with a similar but familiar term.

One of the commonest forms of corruption is *aphesis*, which is the process of the 'gradual and unintentional loss of a short unaccented vowel at the beginning of a word'. (*OED2*) *Cute* is an aphetic form of *acute*; *longshore* is the truncated form of *alongshore*. This explains the American usage *longshoreman* for our *stevedore*. *Stevedore* is itself an aphetic adaptation of the Spanish *estivador*, which drives from *estivar:* to stow a cargo.

Likewise, *sample* is an aphetic form of *example*; *backward* is an aphetic form of *abackward*; and *vanguard* was once *avauntguard*, from which *avant-garde* also derives.

Ninny is an aphetic and abbreviated form of *an innocent.* More recently, we have *squire* from *esquire, specially* for *especially.* In the language of the law, several ambiguous forms survive: *vow* and *avow; void* and *avoid.*

The *goanna* was originally the *iguana.* The *opossum* is now the *possum.* However, it is difficulty of pronunciation which gives us *bandicoot* from the Telugu word *pandi-kokku,* meaning *pig-rat.* (The pandi-kokku is a very large, very destructive Indian rat, the size of a cat. The Australian bandicoot is a different species, but somewhat resembles the Indian rat.)

The process also happens in reverse, by which the original form takes on an additional letter, typically the *n* from the indefinite article. An example of this is *apron,* which originally was *a naperon.* Its connection with *napery* and *napkin* is obvious. Equally obvious is the spoken sound of *a naperon* coming to be spoken as *an apron.* It is odd that we do not say *apkins,* specially since most of us use them more often than we use aprons.

Another example is *orange,* which comes originally from the Arabic *naranj;* in Persian, it was *narang* or *naring;* in late Sanskrit, *naranga;* in Hindi, *narang.* The Italian was originally *narancia,* but is now *arancia.* The Spanish is still *naranja.*

That hallowed hero of the sporting arena, the *umpire,* used to be the *numpire.* The word comes from the Old French *non pair*: 'not equal'. Its earliest recorded spelling in English was *noumpere* (so spelled in 1364, and also in Wyclif's Bible, 1420). The corrupted form emerged soon afterwards, and went through a variety of spellings during the next 200 years (*owmpere, ovmper, ompar, umpere, vmppere, umpeer, umper, unpar, umpyer, impier, umpyre*), until it stabilised on the current spelling in about the seventeenth century.

We have a much more recent expression of closely similar derivation: *au pair*. It has not quite yet become naturalised in English. It means literally *on equality* or *on equal terms*. Its first recorded use in English dates from the late nineteenth century:

> **1897** *Girl's Own Paper* 16 Oct. 'An arrangement ... frequently made is for an English girl to enter a French, German or Swiss school and teach her own language in return for joining the usual classes. This is called being *au pair*.'

Examples of other agents of word-corruption abound. The Australian *plonk*, meaning cheap wine, comes from the French *vin blanc*, notwithstanding that it equally (or more frequently) refers to red wine or other liquor.

That great and traditional accompaniment to festive occasions in Australia, the *saveloy*, is a corrruption of the French *cervelas:* a highly seasoned, cooked, and dried sausage. We have corrupted the thing as much as we have corrupted the word which signifies it.

That fabric so loved by American tourists, *seersucker*, is an East Indian corruption of Persian *shir o shakkar:* literally, 'milk and sugar'.

The strange glow which sometimes surrounds a ship's mast at sea is called *Saint Elmo's fire*. This is a corruption of

Saint Erasmus, an Italian bishop who was martyred in 303 AD. He was the patron saint of Mediterranean sailors. It comes to us by way of *Sant Ermo, San Telmo*, and *Sant Helmo.*

Devotees of square dancing or Nashville sounds will recognise *do-si-do* as one of the caller's instructions. It is a corruption of the French *dos-à-dos*, and describes a figure in which two people pass around each other, back to back, and return to their places.

The word *nickname* has always seemed a curious construction. It has been suggested that it is an invocation of the Devil ('Old Nick'). However, that piece of folk etymology is wrong. Originally, it was an *eke-name.* To *eke* is to supplement; so the person who *ekes out a living* doing odd jobs is supplementing their other income. It is widely misused. An *eke-name* is a supplementary name. By the fifteenth century, its corrupted form was emerging: the *OED2* gives an instance from 1440 which refers to '*neke name* or *eke name*'.

Real estate agents, who offer penthouses for sale as the height of luxury living at the very top of a building, might be forgiven for not knowing that it was originally a lean-to or covered-in walkway. *Penthouse* combines the effects of several agents of change. Its earlier form is *pentice,* which comes from Old French; and *apentis* and *apendis*, from medieval Latin *appendicium,* 'a small sacred building dependent upon a larger church'. From that original meaning and form, it came to mean any small dwelling attached to a larger one. In 1592 the records of the Manchester Court Leet refer to 'setting upp a slated pentis or hovell'. The recent development of the word may be discerned from the following quotations from *OED2*:

1921 *Country Life* Apr. 65/1. Two of the elevators were designed to run to the roof, where a pent-house … was being built.

1937 *Sunday Dispatch* 28 Feb. 2/7. You all know from American lyric writers that a pent-house is a thing stuck on a roof. It may comprise one or two floors.

1945 E. Waugh *Brideshead Revisted* i. viii. 194. They're going to build a block of flats, and … Rex wanted to take what he called a 'penthouse' at the top.

COLLECTIVE NOUNS

◆

Without a moment's reflection, we refer to a *school* of fish, a *flight* of stairs, a *host* of angels, or a *pod* of whales. The italicised words are nouns of assemblage or nouns of company. They are sometimes called collective nouns or nouns of multitude. However, I think those expressions are better reserved for such words as *majority*, *group*, and *collection*, which all have implicit an inherent sense of number or multitude.

There are not many nouns of assemblage in general use. Those which are in use sound so natural to the ear that we rarely pause to reflect how easily idiom settles into consciousness. The strangeness, and sometimes the poetry, of some nouns of assemblage is only seen clearly when we encounter some of the rarer examples of the species.

In 1486 *The Book of St Albans* was published. There is a certain amount of mystery surrounding it. It is thought to be the work of Dame Juliana Barnes, who in turn is thought to have been the daughter of Sir James Berners: spelling was very unstable until Johnson's time, so their surnames are quite possibly variants of the same name. *The Book of St Albans* was also known as *A Treatyse Perteynynge to Hawkynge, Huntynge and Coote Armiris* (A Treatise Pertaining to Hawking, Hunting and Coats of Arms). It contained a great deal of practical information about those subjects, including reference to the correct nouns of assemblage for the creatures and persons likely to be of interest to those for whom the book was intended. It was republished in 1496 by Wyncken de Worde with an additional section on *Fysshynge*.

The *OED2* has 856 quotes attributed to *The Book of St Albans*. It was clearly a book to be accorded some respect. Chief among the purposes for which it is quoted in the *OED2* is its collection of nouns of assemblage. It includes those which are in common use: *colony* of ants, *flock* of sheep, *litter* of pups, *herd* of cattle, *school* of fish. It also has some which catch at the corners of memory: *skein* of geese (when in flight; on the ground, a *gaggle* of geese), *brood* of hens, *clutch* of eggs, *string* of ponies, *plague* of locusts, *bevy* of beauties, and *band* of men.

The real splendour of the *Book of St Albans* lies in its collection of nouns of assemblage which are no longer heard. Some were used as recently as 1906, in *Sir Nigel* by Sir Arthur Conan Doyle. Their passing is probably due to the fact that not many people nowadays do very much *hawkynge* or *huntynge*, although *fysshynge* is still popular. Still, if most know *herd* of elephants, why forget *skulk* of foxes? If we naturally speak of a *pride* of lions, why do we not recall a *hover* of trout?

Although political correctness may dissuade us from talking of a *bevy* of beauties (since compliments are demeaning and condescending, as are insults), it was Dame Juliana who recorded in 1486 the usage *bevy* of maidens. It must be added that she also gave *bevy* as the word for a group of roes, quails, or larks. (For those who baulk at the *s* on *quails*, *OED2* gives quotes from Coverdale, 1535; Cornwallis, 1601; and Otway, 1684 supporting the usage).

Less contentious, and more evocative, are a *charm* of finches, a *drift* of hogs, an *exaltation* of larks, and a *bouquet* of pheasants. This last is an example of how specific some of these terms could be. It refers specifically to a group of pheasant as they break cover in front of the beaters. It derives from the french *bouquet* (little wood), which in turn comes from Italian *bosco* (wood) and *boschetto* (little wood). Our word *bush* is cognate with *bosco*. The original meaning of *bouquet* is the sense still retained in *a bouquet of flowers*. By extension, it refers to the perfume of the flowers, and by further extension to the 'nose' of a wine. So originally a *bouquet of pheasants* naturally evoked the sight of pheasants rising from the bushes ready to be shot at.

Birds must have been very important to the English gentry of the fifteenth century. They had nouns of assemblage for many different types: a *murder* of crows, a *rafter* of turkeys, a *fall* of woodcocks, a *murmuration* of starlings, a *dule* of doves, a *cast* of hawks, a *deceit* of lapwings, an *ostentation* of peacocks, an *unkindness* of ravens, a *host* of sparrows, a *congregation* of plovers, a *mustering* of storks, a *flight* of swallows, a *watch* of nightingales, a *parliament* of owls. How much more drab is our language now, as we refer to virtually any group of birds as a *flock* or a *flight*. A flight is also the word for a company of angels: 'Good-night, sweet prince, and flights of angels sing thee to thy rest.' (*Hamlet* V ii)

More surprising yet is the fact that *The Book of St Albans* records nouns of assemblage for a range of animals which would not form part of the ordinary landscape of even the wealthy nobility of fifteenth-century England. So it includes a *pod* of seals, a *gam* of whales, a *sloth* of bears, a *gang* of elk, a *crash* of rhinoceroses, a *barren* of mules, a *shrewdness* of apes, and a *route* of wolves.

Nor is *The Book of St Albans* confined to *byrdis* and *beystis*. It records the approved nouns of assemblage for all manner of humankind. Many of the terms are self-explanatory; others give an oblique insight into the way various occupations were seen: a *school* of clerks, a *sentence* of judges, an *eloquence* of lawyers, a *subtlety* of sergeants (at law), a *prudence* of vicars, an *obeisance* of servants. For opacity it is hard to pass the following: a *cutting* of cobblers, a *bleach* of suitors (another word for cobblers), a *misbelieving* of painters, and a *worship* of writers.

Colourful ideas sparkle in all of these. Perhaps some of them can be rescued from oblivion. Others must be left under the dust of centuries. Dame Juliana was apparently not one of the Sisters, since she records a *superfluity* of nuns, a *herd* of harlots, a *gaggle* of women, and a *scolding* of seamstresses.

Just as we mistreat some words by ignoring and forgetting them, so we mistreat others by misusing them. With some, the effect of continuous misuse is a permanent change of meaning. With others, it is a prolonged period of irritated confusion. In the end, popular misuse generally prevails. Of the many words in this state of ambiguous confusion, there are three which are currently misused even by people who otherwise use the language with care and skill: *fulsome, ilk,* and *eke.*

Fulsome has one current meaning: 'offensive to normal tastes or sensibilities, disgusting, repulsive or odious; in relation to flattery, grossly excessive or nauseatingly fawning'. Its obsolete meanings are closer to the meaning suggested by its form: *abundant or copious* (1583); and *growing abundantly, rank* (1633). By 1678 it was used in the sense of *overgrown or corpulent*; simultaneously, it took on the sense of *sickening to the taste, nauseating* (1601–1743). It is now most often seen in the expression *fulsome praise*. So used, it is no compliment.

Ilk is generally used as a noun: 'We don't want people of his ilk in this group' — that is, of his sort. In fact, it is a pronoun and means *same*. Two factors have led to its being almost universally misused: first, it can be used absolutely ('more of that ilk' = 'more of the same'). Secondly, it is commonly seen in the titles of Scottish and Irish gentry (*Guthrie of that ilk: Guthrie of Guthrie*). Since most Australians have little cause to be interested in the niceties of Celtic titles, and since the grammatical form suggests something like *Cameron of that clan*, the error takes root. Its erroneous use was further cemented by Ogden Nash in the couplet:

The cow is a creature of bovine ilk
One end moo; the other end milk

Eke is a more complex case. It is most often seen in the phrase *eke out a living* (as discussed in the previous chapter), and is generally intended to convey the notion of scratching along with very little. While not strictly wrong, it is a special case of the more general meaning *to supplement*. Originally, a person would *eke out a livelihood* by doing odd jobs: the odd jobs supplemented whatever other income was available. Likewise, a person would *eke out a speech* with a bit of rhetorical padding.

THE DEVELOPMENT OF LANGUAGE

———◆———

The use of language to communicate ideas is the defining characteristic of the human species. Language is so much a part of our mental landscape that we rarely recognise how extraordinary it is.

The human race has achieved many remarkable things — we have discovered most of the basic principles that make the physical universe what it is. Euclid's geometry, Newton's mechanics, Einstein's relativity, and Planck's quantum mechanics are all discoveries that cast light on the inner workings of the physical world and which, in their own realms, are triumphs of the human intellect.

The capacity for language stands apart from these: it is neither inherent in the physical universe, nor a principle waiting to be discovered. Rather, language is mankind's own invention.

How language evolved is a matter of speculation. It is tempting to think that the same neural architecture that permits or encourages language may also be associated with other forms of communication such as music and art. It is a striking fact that all human societies about which anything is known have this in common: they have developed language, music, and the visual arts.

At their foundation, each of these activities has a common core: the desire to communicate. Painting, sculpture, music, and words are different modes of communication. It is interesting that the other senses — touch and smell — have not developed into significant modes of communication. Even though the sense of smell is governed by a much more ancient part of the brain than language, and must once have been very important to humans, it has not developed the sophisticated and subtle communicative powers of speech and vision. (Those who are interested to pursue this line of speculation would enjoy *Perfume* by Patrick Susskind — a book that convincingly portrays a person for whom the sense of smell is more developed and more powerful than speech.)

Given an impulse to communicate, and given vocal organs capable of a range of sounds, it remains profoundly mysterious that language has evolved in a way that permits subtle and abstract ideas to be communicated with great accuracy. It is one thing to postulate the development of verbal signs which denote such things as *danger*, *pleasure*, *dinosaur*, or *tree*. It is much more difficult to explain the intellectual process which enables humans to conceive, understand, and use verbal tags for such abstract notions as *love, philosophy, probability, mortgage, heaven,* and *metaphor.*

The puzzle becomes even more teasing when you take into account the suggestion that language and experience are deeply inter-related, and in complex ways. Aldous Huxley and others have postulated, convincingly I think, that experience generates language, but that language moderates experience. So the Inuit are said to have 16 different words for snow and to distinguish 16 different sorts of snow at a glance, because their experience makes the distinctions useful. We, who have only one word for snow (skiers have several more), have some difficulty in perceiving the differences between various types of snow, because we do not have the linguistic tags to mark the distinctions.

Edward de Bono did some interesting experimental work in this area. He showed a group of students various simple diagrams which they had to describe unambiguously in words. The diagrams were all capable of being resolved into I-beam shapes. The I-beam quickly became the fundamental unit of description.

De Bono then produced a diagram that, although similar in appearance to the others, was not wholly composed of I-beam shapes: it had some T shapes and some L shapes in it. The students, who had become adept at describing the diagrams in words, were incapable of completely describing this new set of diagrams. Their experience in the tests had taught them the language of the I-beam, but that same language prevented them from perceiving similar, but different, configurations.

As a matter of common experience, it is difficult to form

and manipulate an idea for which we have no verbal tag. Most professional jargon and private codes are an attempt (whether conscious or not) to assign verbal tags to ideas or experiences that have a shared relevance within the limited group.

Huxley speculates that language is a record of past experience which limits future perception (see *Adonis and the Alphabet*). His theory is supported by those who have studied Einstein. Einstein did not speak until he was five years old. He was thought to be a backward child, which turned out to be a pessimistic assessment. However, it has been suggested that his late development of language enabled him to develop more highly than most an ability to think abstractly rather than verbally. This fact has been put forward as an explanation of his ability to conceive his theory of relativity, which has no connection with ordinary experience.

Whether that is true or not, it is important to recognise the link between experience, language, and perception. While it is easy to see how verbal tags such as *noise* or *me* or *water* can be developed and shared with little risk of misunderstanding, it is not self-evident that useful tags for abstract ideas will be universally effective in communicating unambiguous ideas. Take two very different examples. If you and I agree that a letterbox is red, can either of us be sure that the internal physiological experience that we both identify as *red* is the same? All we can be sure of is that we agree to call the same external phenomenon by the same name. It may be that my internal experience of *red* matches your internal experience of *middle C played on a piano*. Timothy Leary's experiments with LSD demonstrated, if nothing else, that the link between external stimulus and internal experience is variable.

If we cannot be confident that *red* means the same for you and me, how is it possible that we can agree on the meaning of words whose intended signification involves one or more layers of metaphor? Suppose you asked a group of people to explain the meaning of: *bourgeois, democracy, interest, industry, culture,* and *communism.* What level of agreement would you expect if the people asked to explain the words were a Russian worker, an English conservative politician, an Eskimo, a biologist, and a factory owner?

It is almost certain that each would have an understanding of each word coloured substantially by personal experience and circumstances. The differences between their respective understandings of the words are likely to be substantial.

Oliver Wendell Holmes once said:

A word is not a crystal, transparent and unchanging, it is the skin of a living thought and may vary greatly in color and content according to the circumstances and time in which it is used.

Those of us who use language as our principal tool of trade would do well to bear this in mind. The communication of an idea is not complete, and not useful, unless the meaning received corresponds with the meaning intended.

DOCUMENTS

———◆———

Lawyers love documents. The traditional image of a lawyer is that of a pasty-looking gent (always male), slightly hunched (from long hours of reading), wearing glasses (all that reading …) at a desk piled high with papers — affidavits, writs, indentures, deeds, titles, charterparties, briefs bound in pink ribbon, documents with wax seals and ribbons — all set against a backdrop of bookcases filled with leather-bound tomes. His mind appears to be scheming and dreaming some complex rigmarole with which to baffle lay people.

Not only do we love documents; we have many different words for them, as the previous paragraph illustrates.

Our commonest word for a thing with writing on it is *document*. It comes immediately from the Latin *documentum*: a lesson, proof, instance, or specimen. Ultimately, it comes from the Latin *docere*: to teach (*docile* originally means ready and willing to be taught). From the original meaning of lesson or proof, it came to mean 'something which serves to instruct or prove', then 'something written containing proof or other information about any subject'.

The original pedagogical meaning of *document* is preserved in one sense of the related adjective, *documentary*. When *documentary* is used as an adjective, it simply means *of or pertaining to a document*; but when it is used elliptically as a noun, '*a documentary*' (on television/radio) it generally means a broadcast with an educational purpose. Oddly, this use of *documentary* seems to be confined to modes of instruction that do not rely on documents, although it picks up the original connection with teaching. When a documentary series on television results in the inevitable book available at bookshops, the book of the series is not called a documentary book.

An affidavit is a statement made in writing, confirmed by the maker's oath, and intended to be used as evidence. It is a modified form of *fidem dare* — to make loyalty — by way of the now-obsolete word *affy*. *Affy* means trust or reliance. It has one or two living relatives: *affiance* (confiding or having faith in a person) and, by extension, *fiancé(e)*.

Writ is much more obvious: it comes from *writing*, and originally meant anything written; but, since the seventeenth century, it has been limited in use to scriptural writings (holy writ) and in law as a written command, precept, or order.

Most lawyers remember that an *indenture* is originally a parchment that has been cut into two or more pieces. In times before word processors, photocopiers, or carbon paper, parties to an agreement faced a practical difficulty in ensuring that the counterparts of the original document were genuine. An early, and practical, arrangement was to write the text of the agreement twice on the same piece of parchment, and then divide it into two parts with a wavy or notched cut. Only the original pieces would fit together perfectly. The indented edges are a natural explanation of the name, which comes ultimately from the Latin word for *tooth*.

Another document with the same origins but a different name is a *charterparty*. It is originally a *carta partita*: a charter that has been divided into several parts. Traditionally it was cut with an indented line, in the same manner as an indenture. In modern times it came to refer specifically to the charter or deed between owners and merchants for the hire of a ship. In Latin, a *charter* (*carta*) is simply a piece of paper; later, in special use, it was a deed, then a written document delivered by the sovereign or legislature, of which Magna Carta is the best-known example. The corresponding portions of an indenture or charterparty are *counterparts*.

It is not obvious that the party of charterparty has anything to do with the party in litigation, but they have the same origins: the idea of division. The Latin *partitum* meant 'that which is divided, shared, or allotted'. In English, it originally signified a division of a whole, a portion. From there it enlarged to encompass 'Those who are on one side in a contest, etc., considered collectively' (as in litigation) and 'a number of persons united in maintaining a cause, policy, opinion, etc., in opposition to others who maintain a different one' (as in a political party).

For some odd reason, people often refer to learned books as *tomes*. Generally this is to be understood as a literary flourish to please and impress. *Tome* comes from the Greek for *volume*, specifically one volume from a larger set. The Greek root *tom-* means slice or cut. In the laboratory, a *microtome* is used for the purpose of taking thin slices off a specimen for examination. Thus the ingenious, but now commonplace, CAT scanning technology is (in its full glory) Computerised Axial Tomography, because it produces images of axial slices through the subject. Likewise surgical operations which involve cutting something out: *gastrectomy*, *hysterectomy*, *lithotomy*, etc; and, of course, the branch of medicine which is learned by cutting up bodies is *anatomy*.

Less obviously, *atom* comes from the same root, meaning *not able to be cut or divided*. Even more remotely, *epitome* in the original Greek is an incision into, or an abridgement of, something; and in English is a summary or condensed account. Tomes, however, are rarely noted for their brevity; a *concise tome* would be thought a contradiction in terms.

Even *rigmarole* has its etymological origins in a form of document. It is a corruption of *Ragman Roll*, a scroll on which the Scottish gentry and nobility subscribed (rather unwillingly) their loyalty to Edward I in 1291–1296. These scrolls bore the proud and glossy seals of all who executed them, having embedded in them the ribbons once thought essential to the dignity, if not the efficacy, of deeds. When the rolls are fully furled up, the ribbons protrude at odd points, giving them a certain shabby chic.

At the time Edward was on his voyage of conversion, there existed a game called Ragman. The main piece of equipment was a scroll which contained a series of short narrative descriptions of various personality traits, rather like the thumbnail sketches that keep readers of horoscopes satisfied. Each character trait had a length of string attached to it, so that, when the roll was fully furled, the strings would protrude from the edges. Each player would take hold of a piece of string and, when the roll was unfurled, the players would read the personality trait at the other end of their piece of string. It must have been tremendously entertaining for all, but sadly the game has fallen into obscurity, along with bagatelle and maypole dancing. Perhaps it was suppressed. Ragman was also a convenient, but illegal, form of gaming: one or more strings were associated with prizes, and players paid to take a string.

In any event, the rolls compiled by Edward looked rather like the playing equipment used in Ragman. Thus, it is thought, the rolls came to be called Ragman Rolls. When opened, the Ragman Rolls contained wordy acts of homage and fealty, all unconnected save for the subject of their feigned admiration, Edward I. By early in the eighteenth century, Ragman Roll had become rigmarole, and meant a succession of incoherent statements; an unconnected or rambling discourse; and a long-winded harangue of little meaning or importance. The original Ragman Rolls are preserved in the Record Office, London.

A *rigmarole*, by definition, is not brief. A *brief*, by definition, should not be a rigmarole. *Brief* is from Latin *breve*: a short catalogue or summary. *Brief* also came to mean a letter, especially a letter of authority. In German it is the common word for letter.

A brief is, or should include, a summary statement of the case in which counsel is retained. In America it is the summary of argument filed with a court. In the US Supreme Court, where oral argument is limited to 30 minutes for each party, the brief is a summary of the entire argument, which must 'be concise … and free from burdensome, irrelevant, immaterial and scandalous matter'. In response to a complaint by Justice Clarke that some briefs exceeded a thousand pages, the 1980 rules imposed a 50-page limit.

DOUBLESPEAK

———◆———

In 1755 Samuel Johnson published his *Dictionary of the English Language*. In the preface, he laments the chaotic state of the language:

> When I took the first survey of my undertaking, I found our speech copious without order, and energetick without rules; wherever I turned my view, there was perplexity to be disentangled, and confusion to be regulated ...

He despaired at the scope and futility of his task:

> It is the fate of those who toil at the lower employments of life, to be rather driven by the fear of evil, than attracted by the prospect of good; to be exposed to censure, without hope of praise; to be disgraced by miscarriage, or punished for neglect, where success would have been without applause, and diligence without reward.

Among these unhappy mortals is the writer of dictionaries; whom mankind have considered, not as the pupil, but the slave of science, the pioneer of literature, doomed only to remove rubbish and clear obstructions from the paths of Learning and Genius, who press forward to conquest and glory, without bestowing a smile on the humble drudge that facilitates their progress. Every other authour may aspire to praise; the lexicographer can only hope to escape reproach, and even this negative recompence has been yet granted to very few.

For the next 170 years, things went on much as before, although we dropped long *S*s and terminal *k*s, and the Americans spiralled off into their own idiosyncrasies.

What Johnson had tried to do for orthography and etymology, Fowler attempted for grammar. In 1926, Henry Watson Fowler brought forth one of the quirkiest books on grammar and style ever published in the English language. *Modern English Usage* combines erudition and grumpiness in a way unrivalled since Johnson. Fowler set out to expose error and ridicule folly, and his manifest irritation is only partly explained by the narrow diet of news available on Guernsey. He understood the difficulty of his task. Under the heading 'Sturdy Indefensibles' he wrote:

Many idioms are seen, if they are tested by grammar or logic, to express badly, and sometimes to express the reverse of, what they are nevertheless well understood to mean. Good people point out the sin, and bad people, who are more numerous, take little notice and go on committing it; then the good people if they are foolish, get excited and talk of ignorance and solecisms, and are laughed at as purists; or, if they are wise, say no more about it and wait …

These grumpy old men of the English language, Johnson and Fowler, concentrated on rules — grammar, orthography, and usage — without too much concern about the purposes for which language was deployed. Love poems or business letters, history or journalism: for them it was all grist for the mill or, as we might say nowadays, input.

Twenty years after the first edition of *Modern English Usage*, George Orwell took the subject a step further. His message was delivered both as an essay, 'Politics and the English Language' (1946), and as a novel, *1984* (1948). Despite his brevity — 'Politics and the English Language' is an essay of only 5,000 words — and his tart astringency, we quickly forgot his message.

It is astonishing that so soon after Orwell showed the stage tricks used by the main offenders, those tricks continue to work. We sit, most of us, like captivated schoolchildren in a sideshow alley, spellbound as the hucksters of language deceive and dissemble. And while we know from Orwell how the tricks are done, we are nonetheless beguiled.

Orwell wrote of the misuse of language by politicians:

A mass of Latin words falls upon the facts like soft snow, blurring the outline and covering up all the details. The great enemy of clear language is insincerity. When there is a gap between one's real and one's declared aims, one turns as it were instinctively to long words and exhausted idioms, like a cuttlefish spurting out ink.

Whereas language was once used as a rapier, it is now used as mustard gas. Corporate mission statements, whilst a harmless idea in themselves, nowadays communicate no intelligible idea more sophisticated than motherhood and apple pie.

Outside the realm of high art, language is intended to convey meaning. Ideally, it should do so accurately. Some writers and speakers betray these ideals, and use language as a sham to mask an intellectual void; or worse, as a stalking horse for quite different ideas that they dare not acknowledge.

The world is awash with examples of the first sort — empty rhetoric dressed up in the finery of Rococo elegance, vacuous new-age gush, or the yawning post-modern fashion of abstraction piled on abstraction — all devoid of real content. These are the empty calories, the fast food of modern discourse. They are the staple of cheap magazines, talk-back radio, and art criticism.

More interesting is the second sort: speech that serves to disguise the thing described. Depending on circumstances, it may be called tact or diplomacy or doublespeak or lying. The proper description depends on the speaker's purpose.

Tact sets out to avoid giving offence. It suppresses or disguises an unhappy truth to spare the feelings of another. It is a down-payment on future favour. It is falsehood in the service of kindness. When tact is lifted from the personal to the national scale, it is called diplomacy.

Euphemism does not directly suppress the truth, but disguises it by substituting gentle words for harsher ones. Its success is limited in the long-term because the euphemism is readily identified with the underlying idea and takes on the colour of that idea. This process is readily seen in the progression of euphemisms regarding universal bodily functions. For example: water closet–WC–lavatory–toilet–loo–the Ladies/Gents room–restroom, etc.

The intention of euphemism is benign, if somewhat fey. Its excesses of delicacy inspired Dr Bowdler to strip Shakespeare of any questionable content. Bowdler's Shakespeare was published in 1818 — before the Victorian age, let it be noted — and was probably influenced by the attitudes which spawned Mrs Grundy. In Morton's play *Speed the Plough* (1798), Mrs Grundy was the neighbour whose narrow and rigid views about propriety were a tyranny for her neighbours.

Tact is kind; diplomacy is useful; euphemism is harmless and sometimes entertaining. By contrast, doublespeak is dishonest and dangerous. In his closing address at the Nuremberg trials, US prosecutor Robert Jackson said:

> Nor is the lie direct the only means of falsehood. They [the Defendants] all speak with a Nazi double talk with which to deceive the unwary. In the Nazi dictionary of sardonic euphemisms 'final solution' of the Jewish problem was a phrase which meant extermination; 'special

treatment' of prisoners of war meant killing; 'protective custody' meant concentration camp; 'duty labor' meant slave labor; and an order to 'take a firm attitude' or 'take positive measures' meant to act with unrestrained savagery.

The war in Vietnam produced such doublespeak expressions as:

Collateral damage: killing innocent civilians
Removal with extreme prejudice: assassination
Energetic disassembly: nuclear explosion
Limited duration protective reaction air strikes: bombing villages in Vietnam
Incontinent ordnance: bombs that hit schools and hospitals by mistake
Active defence: invasion.

When Jimmy Carter's attempt to rescue American hostages in Iran turned into a catastrophic strategic blunder, he described it as 'an incomplete success'. When Soviet tanks invaded Prague in 1968, the manoeuvre was described as 'fraternal internationalist assistance to the Czechoslovak people'.

Doublespeak uses language to smuggle uncomfortable ideas into comfortable minds. The Nazi regime mastered it; the Howard government has been an enthusiastic apprentice.

When senior politicians speak, it is now essential to listen acutely to appreciate that they are simply staying *on message* while avoiding truth, accuracy or anything remotely approaching an answer to the question they have been asked. Even when they appear to be answering the question, you have to look very closely to see which part of the question they are answering. Remember the skilful evasions of Mr Howard when he was asked a question in parliament by Anna Burke, the member for Chisholm:

> Prime Minister, was the Government contacted by the major Australian producer of ethanol or by any representative of him or his company or the industry association before its decision to impose fuel excise on ethanol?
>
> JOHN HOWARD, PRIME MINISTER: Speaking for myself, I didn't personally have any discussions, from recollection, with any of them.

A document obtained by the Opposition under freedom of information laws recorded a meeting that took place between John Howard and Dick Honan about ethanol, just six weeks before the decision.

But Mr Howard says he spoke the truth; that his answer related to a different part of the question and that he was taken out of context.

The victims of protective reaction air strikes, or incontinent ordnance, or active defence, or fraternal internationalist assistance often flee for safety. A small number of them arrive in Australia asking for help. They commit no offence under Australian or international law by arriving here, without invitation and without papers, in order to seek protection. Nonetheless the Australian government refers to them as 'illegals'. This piece of doublespeak is not just for tabloid consumption: it is official. When the Human Rights and Equal Opportunity Commission held an inquiry into children in detention in Australia, the Department of Immigration and Multicultural and Indigenous Affairs made a submission. That submission was stored on the department's web site. The full web address of the submission showed that it was held in a sub-directory called 'illegals'.

Like all doublespeak, 'illegals' is used for a purpose: these people are immediately locked up without trial. No doubt it seems less offensive to lock up 'illegals' than to lock up innocent, traumatised human beings.

They are also disparaged as 'queue jumpers': a neat device that falsely suggests two things. First that there is a queue, and second that it is in some way appropriate to stand in line when your life is at risk.

When the 'illegals/queue jumpers' arrive, they are 'detained' in 'Immigration Reception and Processing Centres'. This description is false in every detail. They are locked up without trial, for an indefinite period — typically months or years — in desert camps that are as remote from civilisation as it is possible to be. They are held behind razor wire, they are addressed not by name but by number, and they slowly sink into hopelessness and despair.

When the new prison for asylum seekers at Port Augusta is completed it will have, in addition to the usual layers of razor wire, an electrified fence. But in the doublespeak of the

Department of Immigration, these are officially called 'energised fences'. Wait for the energised cattle prods.

When a 'detainee' (doublespeak for prisoner) is removed from a detention centre for deportation, the process is generally done in the dead of night and may involve forcibly tranquillising the person; it is generally done by a squad of guards in costumes reminiscent of Darth Vader. This alarming procedure is sanitised as 'an extraction'.

In the desert camps, dormitories are regularly checked during the night: at 8.00 p.m., midnight, and 4.00 a.m., by shining a torch in the face of each detainee and demanding to see their identification. This is a 'security check'. It also fits within one of the standard definitions of torture.

If detainees are driven to the desperate extreme of suicide or self-harm, the Minister, Philip Ruddock, disparages this as 'inappropriate behaviour' designed to 'manipulate the government'. By that doublespeak, the victim becomes the offender.

On the last sitting day in June 2002, the parliament passed the Migration Legislation Amendment (Procedural Fairness) Bill 2002. The title is one of the most audacious pieces of doublespeak ever to blight the pages of Hansard. The measures affect the ability of courts to review decisions of the Refugee Review Tribunal. The Tribunal does not afford a right of legal representation; its members are short-term appointees; and its decision-making processes are often unfathomable except by reference to government policy. Its proceedings are frequently not fair, nor are they calculated to be. The requirements of natural justice have been driven out by repeated amendment. The Procedural Fairness Bill reduces to vanishing point the scope for judicial review of Tribunal decisions. The Migration Act now practically guarantees procedural unfairness in decisions that have life-and-death consequences.

The truth of our treatment of refugees is deeply shocking. Innocent people are locked up in dreadful conditions and for an indefinite period; they are deprived of sleep and isolated from the outside world; they are forcibly removed as circumstances require. They live behind razor wire and electric fences. Their powerful will to live is gradually eroded until — all hope lost — they are driven to self-harm. The truth is uncomfortable for the major political parties: they conceal it in doublespeak in the hope that it will be alright.

See how we have emulated pre-war Germany, in both action and language. In Nazi Germany (before the concentration camps became death camps), 'undesirables' were 'placed in protective custody' or 'resettled'. In Australia, 'illegals' are held in 'Immigration Reception and Processing Centres' behind 'energised fences', receiving regular 'security checks' and occasional 'extractions'. Their 'inappropriate behaviours' are not allowed to 'manipulate public policy'.

George Orwell might have thought that his great essay of 1946, in which he exposed the deceits and devices of doublespeak, would lose its power once the workings of the phenomenon were revealed. But he would be disappointed. Slick political language is as powerful now as in 1933: it can hide shocking truth, it can deceive a nation, and it can hand electoral victory to the morally bankrupt.

FADING DISTINCTIONS

———————◆———————

The English language has developed haphazardly. Drawing on diverse sources, it has spawned as rich a vocabulary as any known language. The chaos Johnson found, and tried to tidy up, includes many words that have sprung from the same source with meanings that are related but different. For example, *frail* and *fragile* both come from the Latin *fragilis*. They are not synonyms, even though they share the same central idea. 'A frail old man bought a fragile old vase' sounds right. Reverse the adjectives and the resulting sentence would sound distinctly odd. Similarly, we have many words that sound similar but come from different roots and have different, albeit similar, meanings; and we have words from the same root differentiated by various prefixes or suffixes.

Generally, the distinctions between these approximate twins are useful. English has thousands of them: they account in part for its richness and subtlety. Unfortunately, some of these useful distinctions are being rubbed away by careless handling. As the process continues, the language loses a little of its power and subtlety.

Precious (at least to lawyers) is the distinction between *disinterested* and *uninterested*. A person is *uninterested* in a thing if it holds no interest for them; if they prefer to give their attention to other things. So, I am interested in music and sculpture, but I am uninterested in golf and stamp-collecting. To be *disinterested*, however, is to have no stake in the subject matter. Judges should be interested in cases they decide, but they must be disinterested in them. Increasingly, the two words are used interchangeably. It is now unsafe to say 'disinterested' unless you are confident that your intended audience will understand the true meaning. An important distinction is being lost.

Another casualty of the process is the distinction between *incredible* and *incredulous*. *Incredible* is the condition of not being believable. *Incredulous* is the state of mind that does not believe something. The Australian Prime Minister, Mr Howard, asserted in the lead-up to the November 2001 election that he was unaware that reports of asylum seekers throwing their children overboard at sea were untrue. That assertion was incredible; many people were incredulous that he persisted with it. What is *incredible* often induces *incredulity*; the fact that the two things frequently go hand in hand probably explains the confusion. Facts are *incredible* (not believable); people are *incredulous* (not believing).

The battle to save *reticent* from a takeover by *reluctant* is probably lost. A person who is *reluctant* is unwilling, struggles against a thing, resists it. By contrast, a person who is *reticent* is reserved, silent, disinclined to speak. *Reluctant* comes from *re + luctare*: to struggle. *Reticent* comes from *re + tacere*: to be silent.

Another two words often confused for each other are *interpolate* and *interrupt*. *Interrupt* comes from the Latin *rumpere*: to break. With the prefix it has the obvious meaning *break in upon*, or *break off*. *Interpolate* is more subtle, and extends beyond mere interruption. Originally, it meant to polish up, from *polire*: to polish; from which we also get *polite* and *policy*. It soon came to signify altering a book by adding material, especially spurious material. So it was from the mid-seventeenth to the late nineteenth century. But from the late eighteenth century mathematicians had been using it in a more neutral sense. Mathematicians used it to signify the completion of a series of numbers by the introduction of numbers in the unfilled intermediate positions by calculation from those numbers already known. The gravitational pull of scientific use slowly influenced the lay use; so in ordinary speech it came to mean any words, comment, or observation inserted in the middle of other material. It has lost its pejorative connotation, although it may still involve an interruption that is ill-mannered by reason of bad timing.

Another fading distinction — a battle almost certainly lost — is the distinction between *surprise* and *astonish*. Surprise comes from *sur + prehendere*: literally *over + take hold of*. Originally, to overpower the mind or will; then to attack suddenly, or to capture by force; then to come on unexpectedly, to take unawares; then to affect with the emotion of being taken unawares, which approximates its current principal meaning. *Astonish* is cognate with *stun*, but its intensity has gradually diminished. Originally it meant to stun, paralyse, or deaden; then to stun mentally, then to dismay, then to shock. The Coverdale Bible (1535) has 'Be astonished (o ye heauens), be afrayde, and abashed at soch a thinge' (Jeremiah 2:12); the King James version (1611) has 'The people were astonished at his doctrine' (Matthew 7:28). In 1844, Macaulay wrote 'Weymouth had a natural eloquence, which sometimes astonished those who knew how little he owed to study' — a deftly ambiguous comment.

The distinction between *surprise* and *astonish*, at least as lexicographers would have it, is best captured in a story (no doubt apocryphal) about the great lexicographer and pedagogue Noah Webster. It is said that his wife found him embracing their maid. She said 'Noah, I am surprised'. He replied: 'No. You are astonished; it is we who are surprised'.

Astonish may have lost some of its original force, but it is still a strong word. The language needs a word for a similar emotion at a lower pitch. *Surprise* does the job. The distinction remains only in the story about Webster, and he died in 1843.

Confusion between *dysfunctional* and *non-functional* probably comes from the attraction (irresistible to some writers) of new and important-sounding words. *Dysfunctional* crawled out of the swamp of social-science jargon. Its apparent meaning seemed obvious enough, and it quickly became a desirable substitute for the dowdy, familiar *non-functional*. *Non-functional* simply means not able to function;

broken; unserviceable. *Dysfunctional* means functioning badly, functioning in a manner abnormal, or not intended. The distinction is real and useful, and should be preserved, if only to spare us a replacement neologism from social scientists.

The same tendency of some writers to prefer the important-sounding word where it is available probably explains the recent vogue of *epicentre*. When writers wish to place a thing more emphatically at the centre of events, they often refer to it as being 'at the epicentre'. This is plainly wrong, and means quite the opposite of what is intended. The *epicentre* is not some mysteriously intensified form of centrality. On the contrary, the epicentre is *never* at the centre of a thing. The word comes from seismology, where it is used to identify the point on the earth's surface immediately above the centre of a seismic event. By definition, the epicentre is above the true centre: often many miles above it. The Greek prefix *epi-* means *upon*, and is used in many technical words that, because of their obscurity, have avoided the careless treatment received by *epicentre*.

FOSSILS

The English language is constantly changing. Words are imported or invented; words come into fashion and fall from favour. Ideas and circumstances change, leaving some words with no useful work to do. When that happens, the stranded word generally fades into obscurity, with only the lexicographer's *obs.* or *arch.* as an epitaph.

The number of dead and dying words is incalculable. But sometimes an obsolete word survives in an isolated idiom or proverbial usage, like a fossil in the cliff-face. This is curious, because it shows that we retain some memory of the word's meaning, and have some use for it, yet we confine its use to a single, specific context. For example, *betide* is never seen except in the proverbial *woe betide*. To *betide* is to *happen* or *befall*.

Another example is *kith*, used only in the idiomatic *kith and kin*. The *OED* defines it as meaning:

1. knowledge, acquaintance with something;
2. knowledge how to behave; rules of etiquette;
3. the country or place that is known or familiar; and
4. the persons who are known or familiar, taken collectively; one's friends, countrymen or neighbours, in later use sometimes confused with kin.

In its principal meaning of *knowledge of how to behave*, it has the same origins and meaning as the equally obsolete *couth*, which survives only in the negative form *uncouth*.

Hue and cry is often used and often misused as well. *Hue* comes from an Old French word that means *outcry* or *hunting-cry*. The last use of it recorded by the *OED* is in a magazine article dated 1779: 'As soon as M. Lally appeared, a hue was set up by the whole assembly, hisses, pointing, threats and every abusive name.' It is etymologically unrelated to *hue* in reference to colour or complexion, which derives from Old German.

The expression *hue and cry* is interesting in another way, as an example of pairs of words that are commonly used together, but which bear substantially identical meanings. Other examples are *let or hindrance, will and testament, cease and desist, null and void*, and so on and so forth. Where such pairs are found in a legal context, it is often the case that one of the pair is Anglo-Saxon and the other is Norman French. The duplication was, in earlier times, an aid to understanding and a safeguard against the possibility that the nuances of the words in their native languages may not have been identical. The modern, relaxed, approach to legal drafting makes the repetition unnecessary, but some old habits die hard.

Another example of this form of duplication is *part and parcel*. It uses *parcel* in a sense no longer current: *a constituent or component part, something included in the whole.* So, in *Taylor's case* (1676) volume 86 of the English Reports at page 189, which established blasphemy as a common law offence in England, the court held that Christianity was 'parcel of the laws of England; and therefore to reproach the Christian religion is to speak in subversion of the law'.

Brand new is one of very few surviving uses of *brand* meaning *fire*. The same meaning survives in the *branding iron* and, surprisingly, in *brandy*. They all come from the old Germanic *brand* meaning *fire*. In modern German, *gebrannt* means *burned*. In four of his plays, Shakespeare uses the expression *fire-new* where we would say *brand new*. For example, King Lear: '*Despite thy victor sword and fire-new fortune, Thy valour and thy heart — thou art a traitor.*'

Brandy was originally called *brandwine* or *brandewine*, or *brandy-wine*. It meant simply wine which had been treated with fire (that is, distilled). *Brandywine* left its mark not only on innumerable livers, but also on American geography: it gave its name to three frontier towns and a creek in America (see, for example, Mark Twain's *Life on the Mississippi*, 1883), and to a square-rigged American frigate (see Richard Henry Dana's *Two Years before the Mast*, 1840).

Lo and behold is still in current use (although a bit dated), but it is made up of two archaic ingredients. For practical purposes, *lo* and *behold* are never heard separately now, although they are preserved in well-known passages in the

Bible and Shakespeare. Although the second edition of the *OED* gives, as its most recent illustration of *behold,* a quotation from 1860, Upton Sinclair used it many times in *Jungle* (1906), and James Joyce used it in *Portrait of the Artist as a Young Man* (1916).

Bide your time is advice often given, in particular by older people (who understand *bide* only faintly) to younger people, who understand neither the verb nor the sentiment, but get the message. The verb *bide* has a range of meanings, all related and all obsolete. The central idea is *remain, await,* or *endure.* In its last meaning (*endure, put up with, submit to*), it is more commonly seen as *abide,* and is familiar to lawyers from the original form of the undertaking as to damages proffered by a party seeking an injunction.

At first blush uses a familiar word, but plainly not in its familiar meaning. Generally, *blush* is used as meaning '*a reddening of the face caused by shame, modesty, or other emotion*'. But several centuries before Shakespeare teased out that meaning, it meant *a glance, blink, or look* (1340); and by 1620 *an appearance or resemblance.* Although Shakespeare used it a number of times unmistakably intending its new meaning, several of his uses of it are ambiguous, and would make sense if *glance* was understood. For example, in *Henry V* (1599), Henry says: 'We hope to make the sender blush at it.'

But compare this with the following:

> **Somerset:** No, Plantagenet,
> 'Tis not for fear but anger that thy cheeks
> Blush for pure shame to counterfeit our roses,

And yet thy tongue will not confess thy error.
Henry VI (Part 1), 1592

Upon his many protestations to marry me when his wife was dead, I blush to say it, he won me.
All's Well That Ends Well, 1602

Whys and wherefores is more proverbial than colloquial, and its use often betrays a failed attempt at literary distinction. The failure is more striking when it appears that the writer is not aware that the expression is a pleonasm: the words mean the same thing. His most often-quoted (and perhaps misunderstood) use of it is Juliet's cry in *Romeo and Juliet* (1595): 'O Romeo, Romeo! wherefore art thou Romeo? Deny thy father and refuse thy name; Or, if thou wilt not, be but sworn my love, And I'll no longer be a Capulet.'

From this, it seems, some assume *wherefore* means *where*. *Wherefore* simply means *for what reason, for what purpose* — in short, *why*. Shakespeare used it often: 'And if I die no soul will pity me: and wherefore should they …' (*Richard III*) It did not go out of common use until the late eighteenth century.

By early in the nineteenth century, the recorded use of *wherefore* suggests uncertainty about its meaning. Although Charles Dickens uses it in its proper meaning, he puts it in the mouth of his characters with a vague or mistaken sense, for example in *Oliver Twist* (1838):

'Because, my pretty cross-examiner,' replied the doctor: 'because, viewed with their eyes, there are many ugly points about it; he can only prove the parts that look ill, and none of those that look well. Confound the fellows, they will have the why and the wherefore, and will take nothing for granted.'

Meat and drink preserves the original meaning of *meat* as *food*. The *OED* records this usage as late as 1902. The same meaning is also preserved in *mincemeat*, the sweet mash of dried fruits used in Christmas pies (mince pies). Until early this century, *green-meat* was grass or green vegetables given to horses, and *white-meat* was anything made with milk. We still refer unselfconsciously to confectionary or cakes as *sweetmeats*. And when it is said that *one man's meat is another man's poison*, the meaning is plainer, and the proverb makes more sense, when *meat* is understood as *food*.

HAITCH

'I am told on good authority that in schools of a certain denomination, and in those schools only, it is pronounced invariably as *haitch*, an oddity I cannot explain.' (Arnold Wall, *The Queen's English*, 1958).

Perhaps it would be more accurate to say that the pronunciation *aitch* is hard to explain. The pronunciation of the letter *h* is one of Australia's great social shibboleths: not just the way it is sounded as the first letter of a word, but more particularly the way the name of the letter itself is said. Some people say *haitch*; others call it *aitch*.

Although the spirit of our times is generous, forgiving, and tolerant, the choice between *aitch* and *haitch* can cause a good deal of anxiety and even hostility. Generally speaking, *haitch* is used by those educated in that part of the Roman Catholic school system that traces its origins to Ireland. *Aitch* is preferred by the rest. Some apostates deny their origins by abandoning *haitch*; but there is little traffic in the other direction. When I was a child, I was forbidden to say *haitch*; friends who said *haitch* were appalled that I ate meat on Fridays.

It is not at all surprising that the issue is so confused, since the pronunciation of *h*, when used as the initial letter of a word, has changed significantly over the past couple of millenia.

Although nothing much is certain in matters of language these days, the prevailing view, perhaps illogically, supports the pronunciation *aitch*. The *OED2* gives it thus, and does not recognise *haitch* as an alternative. I say this is illogical, because it might be expected that the name of a letter of the alphabet would give a clue to the sound normally associated with it. In this matter, *h*, *w*, and *y* stand isolated from the rest of the alphabet, although the names of *c*, *e*, and *g* represent only the lesser part of the work done by those letters.

The issue is manifested in at least three ways: how is the name of the letter to be said; is the *h* sounded or not before a vowel; does a word beginning with *h* accept *a* or *an* as the indefinite article?

The sound represented by *h* was known in the Semitic, Greek, and Latin alphabets. In the Semitic it was a laryngeal or guttural aspirate, and remained so in the Greek and Latin. It passed from the Latin into the Germanic languages as a simple aspirate — that is, the sounded breath. It has been variously called *ha, ahha, ache, acca,* and *accha.* These earlier forms of the name explain the current form, and are clearly referrable to the sound represented.

In late Latin, and in early Italian and French, the aspirate gradually ceased to be sounded. In Italian, the *h* was progressively dropped in the written form of words, so that it is now absent from words which, in the French, retain it without sounding it: *eretico* (*hérétique*); *storia* (*histoire*); *oribile* (*horrible*); *osteria* (*hôtel*).

In Anglo-Saxon speech, *h* was always sounded, but from the Norman conquest the English pronunciation of words with an initial *h* gradually adopted the French manner; the English language has always been something of a trollop, pursuing advantage where it can. So for hundreds of years, the *h* was seen but not heard in 'proper' speech, at least in words which derive from the romance languages.

If the initial *h* of a noun or adjective is not sounded, the word naturally takes the indefinite article — *an*. At least from the eleventh century, then, it was natural to refer to *an (h)istory, an (h)otel, an (h)our, an (h)onourable woman, an (h)umble person*. The ambivalence of usage survives in words like *hostler/ostler*.

However, from the eighteenth century on, English usage began once more to aspirate the initial *h*. This coincides with the arrival of the Hanoverian monarchs, whose native language had always sounded the *h*. Thus words that had come into English via French began to be said with aspirated *h*s, although the change was gradual and patchy. Published in 1828, Walker's Dictionary says that *h* is always sounded except in *heir, heiress, honest, honesty, honour, honourable, herb, herbage, hospital, hostler, hour, humble, humour, humorous*, and *humorsome*. Since that time, those underlined have also

changed, but in the USA *herb* is still said with a silent *h*.
Abominable was originally *abhominable*, at least from Wyclif's
time, and was explained as deriving from *ab homine*. It lost its
h in pronunciation and then in spelling, and remained
unaffected by the shift in the wake of the Hanoverian kings.

One of the oddest anomalies of this process is *habitué*,
which is an unassimilated French word but which is generally
spoken with a sounded *h*. By contrast, *an (h)abitual liar* is
commonly said with a silent *h*, although it would be odd not
to sound the *h* in *habit*. *Homage* is likewise anomalous.

As the shift back to aspirating the *h* was slow and
illogical, it is not surprising that it provoked uncertainty in the
choice of indefinite article. The choice is made the more
difficult by a dread of dropping an aitch, which in many
circles is a shocking thing if done incorrectly. The unhappy
result is such usages as *an hotel, an historic occasion, an
hypothesis, an heroic effort, an hysterical outburst*, etc. If the *h* is
sounded, the result is silly and indefensible.

The rule is simple enough: a word which begins with a
vowel **sound** takes *an*; a word which begins with a consonant
sound takes *a*. So, *an honest person, an hour, an heir, an unusual
event*, etc; *a hypothetical case, a historic occasion* (but colloquially
an 'istoric occasion), *a useful suggestion*, etc. Before initials, the
choice of article depends on the way the name of the letter is
sounded: a UN resolution, an S-bend, an HB pencil, an X-ray,
an MP. But if the collection of letters is a recognised acronym,
the choice of article depends on how the acronym is said: a
UNICEF official, an UNCITRAL official; a NATO
resolution, a SALT meeting, a HoJo restaurant.

The anguish associated with sounding the initial *h* or not is common to all English-speakers. One case where the *h* has crept in from error and remained is *humble pie*. Most of us have eaten it metaphorically; few have done so literally. It is a pie made from the entrails of a deer — the parts left over when those of higher station have taken what they want. The entrails of a deer are the *umbles*. The dish is *umble pie*. The *h* is an intruder, which preserves the meaning of the phrase, but disguises its origins.

16

HARMLESS DRUDGES

———◆———

Many people regard philology as a dry subject. Not surprisingly, many people assume that all philologists are therefore dry and humourless people. That may well be true for the generality, but in even the most arid desert an oasis can be found.

I have not met many philologists. Those whom I have met have ranged from intellectual stick-insects to crusty pedants. I have read many books written by philologists: a significant number of them are the works of dry and humourless authors. However, there is a surprising number of philologists (or at least published philologists) whose wit crackles and sparkles across the page, and marks them as people who would have been fascinating to meet, if not likeable.

Of all those who write about words, writers of dictionaries seem to have spent their time at the wrong end of the personality queue. Perhaps that is because their purpose is so serious. Perhaps it is because dictionaries are mostly written by committees. The *Oxford English Dictionary*, in all respects a splendid work, is nevertheless soulless and dry. You will read thousands of its pages before encountering anything that could pass as witty, much less flippant. This, notwithstanding that Dr James Murray, who was the guiding spirit of the first edition, was a fascinating, scholarly, and gentle man. Furthermore, because the *OED2* is based on historical principles, it records the facts about the way words have been used, but rarely expresses opinions about that usage. Of course, it characterises words as *obs*, *vulg*, or *archaic*. Likewise, it notes some spellings and usages as erroneous. But these opinions are expressed by use of typographer's marks, or discreet abbreviations in brackets.

Likewise, the *Macquarie Dictionary* (Australia's national dictionary) is neither humorous nor opinionated. The *Macquarie* is not based on historical principles. It cannot claim that excuse for its blandness. Conceived in the 1970s and born in 1981, the *Macquarie* is a monument to post-war permissiveness. It reflects, in language, the tolerance advocated by Dr Spock until he recanted after seeing the living results of a generation of his teaching. It embodies the non-judgemental ideals that elsewhere mask lazy pedagogy ('it doesn't matter what they say or how they say it, as long as they express themselves').

By contrast with the *OED2*'s stoic aloofness, and the *Macquarie*'s non-judgmental blandness, Dr Johnson's *Dictionary* had real character. Johnson wrote the dictionary by himself. Even though he had some limited research support, the writing is his. When published in 1755, his was the first great dictionary of the English language. It was immediately hailed as the greatest dictionary of any living European language. What is remarkable in such a great work of philology is that Johnson's brilliant intellect and salty personality are evident on every page. There are many famous examples. I offer just a few:

> **Patron:** One who countenances, supports, or protects. Commonly a wretch who supports with insolence, & is paid with flattery …
>
> **Oats:** A grain, which in England is generally given to horses, but in Scotland supports the people …
>
> **Foxhunter:** A man whose chief ambition is to shew his bravery in hunting foxes. A term of reproach used of country gentlemen.
>
> **Galleyfoist:** A barge of state; & by our old authors applied to the Lord Mayor of London's barge.
>
> **Goose:** A large waterfowl proverbially noted, I know not why, for foolishness.
>
> **Lexicographer:** A writer of dictionaries. A harmless drudge.

Johnson's definition of *patron* was his coup de grace for his patron Lord Chesterfield. Chesterfield had lent his name, but nothing else, to Johnson's enterprise until shortly before publication when it became apparent that the work was destined for greatness. He then sought credit for it. Johnson wrote to Chesterfield a letter that still stands as a masterpiece of exquisitely polite invective:

MY LORD,

I HAVE been lately informed, by the proprietor of *The World*, that two papers, in which my Dictionary is recommended to the publick, were written by your Lordship. To be so distinguished is an honour, which, being very little accustomed to favours from the great, I know not well how to receive, or in what terms to acknowledge.

When, upon some slight encouragement, I first visited your Lordship, I was overpowered, like the rest of mankind, by the enchantment of your address, and could not forbear to wish that I might boast myself *Le vainqueur du vainqueur de la terre*; that I might obtain that regard for which I saw the world contending; but I found my attendance so little encouraged, that neither pride nor modesty would suffer me to continue it. When I had once addressed your Lordship in publick, I had exhausted all the art of pleasing which a retired and uncourtly scholar can possess. I had done all that I could; and no man is well pleased to have his all neglected, be it ever so little.

Seven years, my Lord, have now past, since I waited in your outward rooms, or was repulsed from your door; during which time I have been pushing on my work through difficulties, of which it is useless to complain, and have brought it, at last, to the verge of publication, without one act of assistance, one word of encouragement, or one smile of favour. Such treatment I did not expect, for I never had a Patron before.

The shepherd in Virgil grew at last acquainted with

Love, and found him a native of the rocks.

Is not a Patron, my Lord, one who looks with unconcern on a man struggling for life in the water, and, when he has reached ground, encumbers him with help? The notice which you have been pleased to take of my labours, had it been early, had been kind; but it has been delayed till I am indifferent, and cannot enjoy it; till I am solitary, and cannot impart it; till I am known, and do not want it. I hope it is no very cynical asperity not to confess obligations where no benefit has been received, or to be unwilling that the Publick should consider me as owing that to a Patron, which Providence has enabled me to do for myself.

Having carried on my work thus far with so little obligation to any favourer of learning, I shall not be disappointed though I should conclude it, if less be possible, with less; for I have been long wakened from that dream of hope, in which I once boasted myself with so much exultation,

My Lord,
Your Lordship's most humble
Most obedient servant,
SAM. JOHNSON.

There can be no aspect of English usage or vocabulary that has not been the subject of countless books by countless philologists. So far as it is possible to form a picture of their authors, faceless behind the torrents of words, it is apparent that the writers are not always as interesting as their subject.

But as with dictionaries, so here there are those whose strong opinions or quirky personality demand attention or even affection. My favourite among these is H.W. Fowler. Fowler was as opinionated and as acerbic as Johnson. *The Oxford Companion to the English Language* says of Fowler:

> Fowler was a gifted amateur scholar ... he remained essentially unaware of the linguistic controversies sweeping through the Universities of Europe and the New World. He did not read the learned journals and books in which scholars ... were propounding the doctrine of prescriptive linguistics. His models were the classical languages of Greece and Rome, modified to suit the facts of the English language as he saw them. The responses of writers and scholars to his work have varied, journalists tending towards praise and even adulation, academic linguists towards caution and even reproof ... (1858–1933).

Fowler's great contributions to philology are four in number: he edited the first edition of the *Concise Oxford English Dictionary*; he edited the first edition of the *Pocket Oxford English Dictionary*; with his brother Frank he wrote *The King's English*; and he wrote *Modern English Usage*.

The structure of *The King's English* is that of a fairly orthodox grammar. However, its contents show nicely that the Fowler brothers were not afraid of expressing their personal views. *Modern English Usage* was planned by the brothers jointly, but it was written by H.W. alone, due to the death of F.G. from tuberculosis contracted during the Great War. In an act of public grace he dedicated *Modern English Usage* to his brother, and touchingly lamented that Frank could not have contributed to the writing of it.

Modern English Usage is nothing if not quirky. It comprises a series of articles, arranged alphabetically: simple enough but for the fact that many of the articles have such idiosyncratic titles that only a person who has read the work would have the slightest idea where to look for information on a particular subject. For example: **Wardour Street** (on quaint and anachronistic language); **barbarisms** (any usage Fowler doesn't like); **battered ornaments** (linguistic flourishes past their use-by date); and **sturdy indefensibles** (usages that are wrong and yet persist, despite the complaints of such writers as Fowler).

Just as the article titles are idiosyncratic, so the contents are unmistakably H.W. Fowler. For example:

Stock pathos. Some words & phrases have become so associated with melancholy occasions that it seems hardly decent to let such an occasion pass unattended by any of them. It is true that such trappings & suits of woe save much trouble; it is true that to mock at them lays one open to suspicion of hard heartedness; it is also true that the use of them suggests, if not quiet insincerity, yet a factitious sort of emotion, & those are well advised who abstain from them.

Split infinitive. The English speaking world may be divided into (1) those who neither know nor care what a split infinitive is; (2) those who do not know, but care very much; (3) those who know & condemn; (4) those who know & approve; & (5) those who know & distinguish.'

Pedantry. May be defined, for the purpose of this book, as the saying of things in language so learned or so demonstratively accurate as to imply a slur upon the generality, who are not capable or not desirous of such displays. The term, then, is obviously a relative one; my pedantry is your scholarship, his reasonable accuracy, her irreducible minimum of education, & someone else's ignorance. It is therefore not very profitable to dogmatise here on the subject; an essay would establish not what pedantry is, but only the place in the scale occupied by the author; & that, so far as it is worth enquiring into, can be better ascertained from the treatment of details, to some of which accordingly, with a slight classification, reference is now made.

The second edition of *MEU* was edited by Sir Ernest Gowers. Unfortunately, he has none of Fowler's spiky opinions, and it has lost some of the personality that characterised the first edition. Robert Burchfield has produced a third edition which, while it is certainly worth having, bears almost no resemblance to the original work.

A contemporary writer, Philip Howard, also shows some of Fowler's striking individuality. With all the confidence of one who worked for *The Times* before Rupert Murdoch took it over, Philip Howard seems the self-appointed angry young man of philology. No one could agree with him all the time, and sometimes he does take liberties, but he is eminently readable.

I do not have the time or the space now for a discussion of Philip Howard; nor of Ivor Brown; nor the gentle Professor Ernest Weekley, MA. Of them, something another time.

Instead, for balance and symmetry, the Australian Fowler: Nicholas Hudson. His *Modern Australian Usage* was published in 1993, appropriately enough by Oxford University Press. Like Fowler, his article headings are unpredictable, and his prejudices are plainly exposed. His writing is splendid — a Bob Ellis of philology. For example:

Repetitions and refreshers. If St Paul had had a keen sense of economy and less sense of theatre, he might have written 'charity ... beareth, believeth, hopeth, and endureth all things'. However, he was repetitious: 'charity ... beareth all things, believeth all things, hopeth all things, endureth all things'.

A second use of repetition is the refresher. The term is borrowed from commerce, where it refers to the sums which have to be fed at regular intervals into time-based devices like parking meters and barristers.

Respect. In utterances starting *Mr Chairman, with respect* ... the phrase *with respect* is a conventional signal that what follows is a dissent from the Chairman's ruling. It is thus a hypocritical euphemism. Nevertheless, the convention which demands it is a good one, giving the Chairman an opportunity to retreat on a specific point while maintaining overall authority.

Ploddery. There is a curious idiolect which is associated, not entirely unfairly, with Mr Plod, the police witness in a court of law, and is hence called *ploddery*. It is noted for pleonasm, for self-conscious use of less common words ... for malapropisms ... and for using everyday words and phrases in ways which, while they are in the dictionary, are not the ways these words are normally used, e.g. *to acquaint with* (= to tell), *to effect* (= to make), *to occasion* (= to cause), *particulars* (= facts).

The other characteristic of ploddery is to construct sentences of quite unnecessary complexity, often starting with adverbial clauses which hang about in the corners of the Court, waiting for a main verb. Some people can do this sort of thing and get away with it. There are radio interviewers whose control of immensely long and complex sentences never ceases to astonish me. Just as I am thinking that they must have lost the thread, the ends are joined up and out comes an immaculate finished garment. Mr Plod, on the other hand, just runs the sentence on and on.

Chastened by that, I end.

17

HOLY WARS

———◆———

President George W Bush has never displayed much sensitivity to the nuances of language. Even its basic rules seem to elude him. Consider a few of his famous blunders while speaking on public occasions, and try to imagine the qualities of his less-considered private discourse:

More and more of our imports come from overseas.

What I'm against is quotas. I'm against hard quotas, quotas that basically delineate based upon whatever. However they delineate, quotas, I think, vulcanize society.

If you're sick and tired of the politics of cynicism and polls and principles, come and join this campaign.

You teach a child to read and he or her will be able to pass a literacy test.

He speaks in semantic near-misses as his grammar lurches from one rough approximation to the next.

During the incumbency of this linguistic torment, the world changed permanently and catastrophically. In the immediate aftermath of the terrorist attack on the USA, President Bush said that America and the rest of the free world would embark on a 'crusade against terrorism'. He soon changed his choice of words. It became a 'war on terrorism'. Bush may not be a master of the language, but his spin-meisters quickly saw that *crusade* had connotations that might give offence beyond the intended range.

Crusade is historically associated with the series of assaults by Christian forces against Muslim control of Jerusalem and the Christian shrine of the Holy Sepulchre. There were eight main crusades, between 1095 and 1270. The disastrous fourth crusade culminated in the sacking of Constantinople in 1204, during which the great library there was looted and destroyed, and the only extant copies of many classical texts were lost to mankind. It was an event of cultural destruction almost unparalleled in history.

Etymologically, Bush's advisors were wise to drop references to a *crusade*. The word came to English via French and derives ultimately from *crux*, the Latin for *cross*. It was variously spelt *croisad*, *croissard*, *croisada*, *crusada*, etc. Specifically it meant a military expedition by the Christians to recover the Holy Land from the Muslims; and, by transference, any military expedition blessed by the church. In short: a holy war. Even for the fundamentalist Bush, this was a bit too explicit.

The equivalent expression in Arabic is *jihad*. The Western world has reacted with understandable alarm when Osama bin Laden declared jihad on various nations, including Australia, which managed to lift itself from safe obscurity to swaggering prominence in a single idiotic gesture. But it was President Bush who first invoked the language of holy wars.

Our headlong rush into conflict has brought into common currency a number of words previously misused or unfamiliar: *mufti*, *fatwa*, *sheikh*, *shah*, and *mullah* among others.

A *mufti* is a canonical lawyer in Islam: he gives decisions on questions of faith. The word is derived from the active participle of *afta*, which is the fourth conjugation of *fata*: to give a decision. A decision so given is a *fatwa*. A *fatwa* may be benign or dangerous according to the subject matter. Most English speakers first heard of a *fatwa* in connection with Salman Rushdie: it had been decided that, because he had written *The Satanic Verses*, he should be killed wherever he could be found. Even those who were immune to the charms of Rushdie's writing thought this was an unreasonable restriction on free speech. This very harsh and public fatwa gave fatwas in general a bad name in the West.

Mufti is commonly used in the West as referring to civilian clothes worn by one accustomed to wear a uniform. It is thought to derive from the passing similarity between the regalia of a mufti and the English affectation of dressing gown, smoking cap, and slippers.

Mullah has various meanings in various parts of the Muslim world. In North Africa, a *mullah* is a king, sultan, or other leader. Further east, and in the Indian sub-continent, a *mullah* is similar to a *mufti*. He is a man learned in theology and sacred law. The Qur'an uses *mullah* in reference to Allah. Thus, it is a word that maps almost perfectly onto the English *Lord*, signifying a position of territorial, legal, or spiritual leadership.

Allah comes from *al ilah*: *al* is the Arabic definite article, and *ilah* is the Aramaic for *God*. The holy book of Islam is the Qur'an. *Qur'an* means 'recitation': it is a recitation of the various teachings of God as received by the prophet Mohammed over the course of 20 years up to his death in 767 AD. Composed of 114 *surahs* (chapters), it is arranged according to length, with the longer surahs first. Since the earlier teachings were rather shorter, the book is arranged, roughly, in reverse chronological order. Incidentally, Islam recognises Moses and Jesus as prophets, and the God of the Qur'an is the same God worshipped by Jews and Christians: the crusades were more an argument about the messenger than about the message.

An essential feature of the teachings in the Qur'an is the importance of unquestioning submission to the teachings of the Prophet. *Islam* means resignation or submission. It is the fourth conjugation of *salama*: 'he was or became safe, secure, or free'; hence *salaam* as a greeting of peace, which is coupled with a gesture of submission. Self-evidently, *salaam* is cognate with the Hebrew greeting *shalom* (peace).

Many Muslim words incorporate the name of Allah:

Allahu akhbar: God is great
Bismillah: (bi'sim illah): in the name of God

Hezbollah (*hezb* = party): party of God, an extreme
Shiite Muslim sect
Inshallah: if Allah wills it, God willing
Mashallah: what God wills must come to pass

Like *mullah*, *sheikh* has meanings which vary with
geography. Its original meaning was 'an old man': specifically a
man of 50 or older. (In times past, age and wisdom were seen as
functionally related. This philosophy was temporarily displaced
when the baby boomers graduated from university, and was
rediscovered when they began to collect their superannuation.
The process continues, with resistance, from Generation X). A
sheikh is the chief of an Arab family or tribe. It is also applied to
heads of religious orders, heads of learned colleges, heads of
towns or villages, to learned men generally. It is also accorded to
those who have memorised the entire Qur'an at whatever age (a
fair achievement, since it is about 300 pages long).

Although closely related in sound and meaning, *shah* is
etymologically unrelated to *sheikh*. S*hah* is Persian for *king*. It
has left one important trace in English. In that most civilised
form of warfare, chess, the game ends when one player places
the opponent's king in a position from which it cannot escape.
The King is not formally taken, but it is unable to move to a
position where it could avoid being taken. The victor
announces 'checkmate'. That triumphant declaration is the
anglicised *shah mat*: the King dies.

The crusade I began with was once a *croissard*, which is
reminiscent of *croissant*. They are not etymologically related,
but there is a connection between them. While *croissade-*

crusade came from Latin *crux* (French *croix*), *croissant* is French for *crescent*. In 1683, Vienna was struggling to survive a siege by the Ottoman Turks. A Pole named Kolscitzky, who was learned in Turkish, came to their rescue. He escaped through enemy lines to reach the Duke of Lorraine, who hurried to relieve the city. The Turks were repelled, and Vienna was saved. Kolscitzky became very popular and famous, and persuaded a baker to produce a sweet bread roll in celebration of Vienna's victory over the Turks. It was shaped like the crescent on the Turkish flag.

We call them *croissants* because at some point the French took ownership of this Polish-Austrian idea. The crescent they imitate refers originally to the new moon as it grows towards the first quarter: the word comes from the Latin *crescere* to grow (from which we also get *crescendo*, and *increase*). As a new moon grows it is a *waxing crescent* moon (a tautology); after the first quarter it is *waxing gibbous* (from the Latin for *hump*); and then full. As the full moon declines, it is *waning gibbous;* then, after the last quarter, it is *waning crescent* (a contradiction in terms).

Incidentally, during his perilous journey Kolscitzky had learned how to make coffee. After the siege ended, he came by a sack of coffee beans abandoned by the retreating Turks. Being the only person in Vienna who knew what coffee beans were for, he opened a café which quickly became famous for the drink, and popular for its croissants. He served the coffee with milk and honey, a precursor of the style now known as Vienna coffee. Although the French stole the croissant, they had the good sense to leave Vienna coffee to the Viennese.

18

IDIOM

———◆———

The English language abounds in idiomatic expressions that, if taken literally, would be utterly confusing to modern speakers. They are a source of endless trouble to people for whom English is a second or temporary language.

For native speakers, the intended sense is learned during childhood by inference from the context: we have no need to analyse *the exception which proves the rule* into its linguistic constituents. We have a vague idea of its meaning, we use it as a conversation filler, and we are untroubled by the thought that an exception should disprove (or at least qualify) a rule.

Prove, in this idiom, does not mean *demonstrate* or *validate*. It has the earlier meaning of *test*. It comes ultimately from the Latin *probare*: to test. This sense was current until late in the nineteenth century, but it survives also in the idiom *the proof of the pudding is in the eating* — that is, a thing is tested by putting it to its intended use.

This expression is often heard in a mangled form

incapable of making sense 'the proof is in the pudding', etc, which serves to illustrate the point that the idiomatic phrase carries a recognised meaning even though the meaning of its constituent parts has been lost. The same sense (and the etymological origins of the word) survives in *proving* a will: if the will is proved, *probate* is granted. In Scottish law, a trial without a jury is still called a *proof*: it is the occasion when the case of the pursuer is tested.

Jot or tittle is an idiom that means any small thing. Curiously, it is close in origin to the idiom which commands attention to every small detail: *dot the i*s *and cross the t*s. (This is one place where the urge to use an inappropriate apostrophe is almost irresistible.) *Jot* is a variant of *iota*, the Greek name for the letter *i*. Iota is still used alone to mean something small, generally by negation: *there is not one iota of evidence*. In exactly the same way, it might be said *there is not a jot of evidence*. The meanings are identical.

The ambivalence between *jot* and *iota* is not surprising: until early in the nineteenth century, *i* and *j* were facets of the same letter. In all editions of Johnson's *Dictionary*, the entry following *hystericks* is *I*, and it contains a discussion of that letter, followed by its meaning as the first-person singular pronoun. The next entry is *jabber*, followed by other words beginning *ja-*. After *jazel* comes *ice*; after *idyl* comes *jealous*, and so on. So it remained in all the editions in Johnson's lifetime. However, the eighth edition, edited by Dr Todd (1818) recognises that *i* and *j* have ceased to be facets of the same thing, and have separated into two different letters. Nevertheless, the eighth edition has the entries for *ice* following the entry for *jazel*. *Iota* and *jot* are small reminders of the way it was.

So a *jot* is simply the letter *i*. A *tittle* is any diacritic mark in text, such as an accent, a cedilla, or a tilde. Nowadays, it refers specifically to the dot above the letter *i*. So reference to *every jot and tittle* is a reminder of the importance of dotting the *i*.

When we speak of *letting the cat out of the bag*, we reveal a secret deceit. This homely expression traces its origins to Elizabethan times, and had become idiomatic by 1760. At country fairs suckling pigs would be offered for sale, but the unsuspecting purchaser would be handed a sack with a cat or a puppy inside. The fraud would be revealed only later when the purchaser let the cat out of the bag. Until that moment, the buyer had *bought a pig in a poke*: a *poke* was a small bag or sack; it is cognate with *pouch* and with the French *poche*. The Scottish equivalent of this expression, significantly — and more accurately — is *to buy a cat in a poke*. The same ruse gives rise to the expression *buy a pup*.

In the Roman Catholic tradition, believers *tell their beads* — that is, count off the beads of the rosary as they say prayers. The expression has a long and interesting history. Originally, a *bede* (or *bead*) was a prayer, or more loosely a wish. It is an Anglo-Saxon word dating from the ninth century. *Bid* is a variant form of *bede*, and one current sense of *bid* still retains its connection with *bede*: when we bid a person farewell we wish them fortune; when we bid a person goodnight, we likewise express a wish for them. This is a different sense of *bid* from that which auctioneers understand. So, to *bid a bead* is a tautology. *Bidding the bedes* simply meant *praying the prayers*. And one of the prayers — *the bidding prayer* — was a list of intercessions on behalf of the various estates and conditions of mankind in special need of divine help.

The French equivalent of *bede* was *priere* (from Latin *preccare*, whence *imprecation*), which gradually altered to *prayer* and ousted the Anglo-Saxon *bede*. By this time, however, *bidding the bedes* was an established usage; and an established habit was to count off the prayers using a string of small globules of glass or semi-precious stones strung together in a circlet. These became symbolic for, and then synonymous with, the prayers they represented, and came to be called *bedes* (from the sixteenth century spelled *beads*). They retained that name even after the metaphysical thing they represented adopted a French name.

As the bedes were said they were *told* — counted — by moving the fingers to the next *bede*. From the tenth to the nineteenth century, *tell* had the meaning *to mention or name one by one, specifying them as one, two, three, etc; hence, to ascertain from the number of the last how many there are in the whole series; to enumerate, reckon in; to reckon up, count, number.* From this we get the *teller* (formerly seen in banks, and currently seen in parliament on a division); and when the *tally* is known we may say there are so many *all told*. Although these forms survive, this sense of *tell* is obsolete.

There once existed in Scotland an order of paupers called the *King's Bedesmen*. They were paid by the king to say prayers for the wellbeing of the royal person and their dominion. These were aligned in spirit to the original beggars: an order of mendicants founded in the twelfth century by Lambert le Begue (he was a stammerer; *begue* is French for stammer). Members of the order were called *Beguins.* The sisterhood he founded were the *Beguines* — Lambert was the first to Begin the Beguine. They lived by seeking alms from others. By the fourteenth century they had come to be called *Beghards*; in the late fourteenth century they attracted the wrath of the Council of Treves, and later that of the Inquisition. Thus were the beggars disgraced.

Oddly, while Pope John XXII attacked the Beghards, he protected the Beguines, who still exist in small communities in the Netherlands.

But, for the most part, what had started as a pure religious calling was brought down in society and in language equally.

19

IRONY

It is common these days to hear *irony* misused — not the device, although that certainly happens, but the word and its adjective *ironic*. So, it has been observed that it was 'ironic that Shane Warne's mother gave him the fluid tablet' which got him into trouble; or that it is 'ironic that bushfires in New South Wales were followed by flash-flooding'.

Irony is a useful word that deserves more care. It may be curious or interesting that his mum's diuretic got Shane Warne into trouble, but it is not ironic. It may be paradoxical, and certainly unfortunate, that one natural disaster is followed rapidly by another of a different sort; but this is not ironic.

Irony draws its name from the Greek *eironia:* 'dissimulation; ignorance purposely affected', which is reflected in the name of a stock comic character in Greek drama called Eiron. Eiron was frequently opposed to the boastful Alazon who, blinded by his own good opinion of himself, failed to notice the skill in Eiron's disingenuous observations, and was defeated. The comic effect of the exchanges between Eiron and Alazon was appreciated by Athenian audiences, who knew in advance that Eiron was cleverer than he seemed and than Alazon noticed.

The central idea of *irony* is the contradiction inherent in words spoken or events depicted. The *OED2* defines it as:

> A figure of speech in which the intended meaning is the opposite of that expressed by the words used; usually taking the form of sarcasm or ridicule in which laudatory expressions are used to imply condemnation or contempt.
>
> A condition of affairs or events of a character opposite to what was, or might naturally be, expected; a contradictory outcome of events as if in mockery of the promise and fitness of things.

And Johnson:

> A mode of speech in which the meaning is contrary to the words: as, 'Bolingbroke was a holy man'.

Socratic irony is the device, adopted by Socrates in imitation of Eiron, of asking seemingly ignorant questions designed to drive dogmatic opponents into logical difficulties. To the audience who understood Socrates' approach, this carried all the enjoyment of seeing the engineer hoist, unwitting, on his own petard. The patient cross-examiner who, by seemingly innocent questions gradually edges her witness into an impossible position, is using Socratic irony. If others in court are aware already of the document or circumstance that will destroy the present witness when the trap is ready, the parallel with Socrates is complete.

Dramatic irony has the audience informed of larger events, unknown to the play's protagonists, so that they proceed in their ignorance towards a fate already prefigured by the audience. In that setting, their words can be made to carry a quite different significance to the audience than they apparently have to the speaker. The same device can be used conversationally, and with just as telling effect. In the last stages of Scott's ill-fated Antarctic expedition of 1912, Captain Oates left the shelter with the comment 'I am just going outside and may be some time'. The circumstances gave his words a very different meaning, which must have been well understood by his companions. Oates' remark is recorded in Scott's journal on 16 March 1912. It is the last entry.

Some will say Oates' comment is an example of *meiosis*, and so it is. *Meiosis* consists in enhancing the effect of what is intended by understatement. The extent of understatement may make *meiosis* and *irony* indistinguishable. *Meiosis* has the effect of emphasis: it does not have the edge or poignancy usually associated with *irony*. *Litotes* is a special form of *meiosis*. It also involves understatement, but couches the statement as the negative or the opposite of what is intended, as in 'no small effort' or 'by no means insignificant'.

Linguistic irony is more concerned with semantic ambiguity than with the contrast between words and circumstances. It is cousin to sarcasm, but is less savage. *Sarcasm* comes from the Greek word meaning *to tear flesh*: it is always unkind. Johnson uses it in his definitions of *lash*, *nip*, and *whip*.

Irony is gentler: the Elizabethan courtier and rhetorician George Puttenham called it 'the drye mock'. So: a very young and inexperienced counsel rose to deliver a plea in mitigation before a stern judge in a serious matter: 'M-m-my poor client … M-m-my poor client …' he stammered. 'Go on, I am with you so far' said the judge. Aristotle said 'Irony better befits a gentleman than buffoonery; the ironical man jokes to amuse himself, the buffoon to amuse other people.'

It is recently fashionable to recognise two other forms of irony: *structural irony* and *romantic irony*. *Structural irony* looks rather like dramatic irony in post-modern clothes. The contradiction is seen between the words spoken in a text and the circumstances being depicted by the text itself. The spectacular maunderings of Sir Joh Bjelke-Petersen were often rich in structural irony, no doubt unintended. Likewise the brilliant BBC TV series *The Office*, in which the principal characters displayed their vanity and foolishness by their own self-inflated management-speak. In *romantic irony* the writer and reader collude in the complete knowledge that their vantage point gives them, and view with wry amusement the folly of the characters within their limited horizons.

Closely related to *irony*, but less often used, is *paradox*. Like *irony*, *paradox* has contradiction at its core. But whereas *irony* finds contradiction between available meanings of a single utterance, or between an utterance and the events to which it relates, *paradox* is concerned with a contradiction in things themselves.

Paradox comes from *para* (against) and *doxos* (opinion). A *paradox* involves a statement that seems true but contradicts observed reality or the opinion or expectation born of experience. Zeno of Elea was famous for his four paradoxes. His *Achilles paradox* proves that the faster runner in a race cannot pass the slower runner. The *arrow paradox* proves that an arrow in flight is actually at rest.

The *liar paradox* was first propounded by Epiminedes in the sixth century BC. 'I am a liar' is truly paradoxical: it is true only if it is false, and false only if it is true.

More recently, *Olbers' paradox* points out that the universe is endless and uniformly populated with stars, so every line of sight must eventually find a star; accordingly, the night sky should be light, as every part of it is occupied by a luminous object.

Because *paradox* is a seemingly exotic word, it is taken and misused by those in search of ornaments for their prose. Fowler calls this tendency *Wardour Street*, after the London street famous for its antique shops: 'Wardour Street … offers to those who live in modern houses the opportunity of picking up an antique or two that will be conspicuous for good or ill among their surroundings.'

'It's quite a paradox how completely we change from conception to death', the *Herald Sun* reported on 9 May 1998. It may be troubling, perhaps, or marvellous, but it is not paradoxical: it is the universal experience that our appearance changes during the course of our lives, and nothing is paradoxical which conforms to universal observation and experience.

From the same root as *paradox* comes *orthodox*:

'Holding right or correct opinions, i.e. such as are currently accepted as correct, or are in accordance with some recognized standard.' (*OED2*)

'Sound in opinion and doctrine; not heretical.' (Johnson)

There are other useful words from the same origin. Unfortunately, they have fallen out of use. As opinions on matters of high importance harden along lines drawn by the saviours of the free world, we may need to revive some.

For our friends:

Homodox (adj): of the same opinion

Pleistodox (adj): holding the opinion of the majority

For our enemies:

Heterodox (adj): of opinions not regarded as correct or accepted

Pseudodox (n): a false opinion

Adoxal (adj): absurd, not according to reason

Cacodox (adj): holding a wrong or evil opinion

And finally, for use on both sides:

Doxastic (adj): depending on or exercising opinion; an object of opinion;

Doxographer (n): one who collects and records the opinions of others.

LEGAL WORDS

———◆———

The effect on the English language of the Norman invasion is well known and easily observed even now. From 1066 until Normandy was lost by King John in 1204, the ruling class in England was composed largely of nobles whose native land was France. After 1204, a sense of allegiance to France became progressively less relevant. By that time, however, a large number of Anglo-Saxon words had been displaced by Norman French equivalents.

Because the Norman rulers were truly a conquering force, they did not assimilate in quite the same way as the Scandinavians had 200 years earlier. Thus, the influence of French on English is greatest where the influence of the ruling invaders was greatest. So, the language of government, law, military leadership, and the baronial table is dominated by French words. The language of the farm, the fields, and the trades shows a healthy survival of Anglo-Saxon words.

In *Ivanhoe*, Sir Walter Scott identified the language

divide between farm and table: the English serfs tended the Anglo-Saxon *boar, calf, cow, bull, deer, ox, sheep, pig,* and *swine.* At table, the Norman overlords ate the French *brawn, veal, beef, venison, mutton, pork,* and *bacon.* (It is tempting to add *ham* to this list. The connection with the French *jambon*: leg and Italian *gamba* is obvious and plausible. However, *ham* existed as *homme* before the Norman conquest, meaning the part of the leg at the back of the knee).

In the language of the law, it is difficult to find words that do not derive from the Norman influence. Apart from obviously French words (*tort, oyez terminer, assize, malfeasance,* and *puisne*), many others are French but are so completely naturalised as to pass unnoticed: *arrest, accuse, acquit, convict, punish, pardon, plead, sue, damage*, and so on.

Indict is a Norman French word. It derives in turn from the Latin *dictare*, to say or declare. So, originally, it was a statement or declaration by which a person was made aware of charges against them. Its use was not confined to the law, however. As late as the eighteenth century, Handel wrote the *Coronation Anthems*, one of which is called 'My Heart is Indicting', the sense of which is that heart-felt sentiments for the new King George are put into words.

Parliament is another obvious Norman French word. It comes from *parlement*: speaking. The Anglo-Saxon word it replaced was *witenangemot*: discussion of the wise men (perhaps circumstances would eventually have forced the abandonment of this word in any event). Although *witenangemot* has not been used since the eleventh century, it has left a small legacy to modern English. The constituent roots are *witan* (wise men) and *mot* (discussion). *Mot* was a variant form of *moot*, a discussion or debate. It survives in our *moot courts*, and in the idiom *moot point*.

It is not uncommon to hear it said that 'the point is moot', with the intended meaning that the point does not arise for debate, especially because it is hypothetical. A *moot point* is one that is debatable or doubtful. It is not accurate to use it as meaning *hypothetical*, although a hypothetical question clearly can be debatable. As a verb, to *moot* an idea is to raise it for discussion.

Another interesting by-product of the French influence on English courts is *culprit*. At least from the time of the *Year Books*, when a prisoner had pleaded not guilty, the Clerk of the Crown would assert the guilt of the prisoner (*culpable*) and announce the readiness of the Crown to prove its charge (*prest d'averrer nostre bille*). This form is found repeatedly in the *Year Books*. The word *prest* was also written as *prist, prit,* and *pret*. It corresponds to the modern French *prêt*: ready. The written record of a trial often used abbreviations for formulaic portions of the proceeding. Thus, it is thought, the formula *culpable: prest d'averrer nostre bille* was abbreviated to *cul.prest* or *cul.prist*. It was later mistaken for a mode of addressing the prisoner. *Culprit* is first recorded as a word in 1678, in the record of the trial of the Earl of Pembroke. The *OED2* gives the following quotation:

> *Clerk of Crown.* Are you guilty, or not guilty?
> *Earl.* Not guilty.
> *Cl. of Cr.* Culprit, how will you be tryed?

Earl. By my Peers.
Cl. of Cr. God send you a good deliverance.

And what about that curious word *premises*, which lawyers and logicians use so often? Normal people speak of *the premises*, meaning the house or other building that concerns them. Logicians speak of *the premises* (or *premisses*), meaning the starting propositions of a syllogism. Lawyers, wanting to summarise all that went before without having to repeat it, say *in the premises* …

They are all the same word, with the same original meaning and, as ever, lawyers use the word in its ancient and proper sense. *Premises* are previous statements or propositions from which a stated conclusion follows. A formal conveyance of real estate begins with a recitation of the parties, a description of the property, and the vendor's title. Lawyers refer to those details later in the deed as *the premises* (as logicians would). Laymen, naturally, take that as a reference to the most important of the premises — namely, the property conveyed.

At least one legal expression in common use, *by-law*, escaped the Norman influence, and survives as a reminder of the earlier Scandinavian influence on English. The Danish *by* and the old Norse *byr* mean *town or settlement*. *By* is found as a suffix in many place names, such as Derby, Normanby, Whitby, Rugby, Kirkby, and so on. It was readily assimilated into Anglo-Saxon because of its similarity to *burg* and (Scottish) *burgh* (English: *borough*). *By-laws* were, and generally still are, the local laws of a town or region.

LITTLE ORPHANS

———————◆———————

Many words are members of a recognisable family, of which the principal members are generally nouns, verbs (and participles), adjectives, and adverbs. So: *a home, to home* (*homing*), *homely*; *a friend, to befriend, friendly*, and so on. The family tree expands when prefixes and suffixes are used as modifiers.

Apart from members of the immediate family, there also arise parallel families, cousins if you will: *friendship* and *friendliness* are both nouns that extend the concept implicit in *friend*; and, in a slightly different way, so do *ellipse* (geometrical shape), *ellipsis* (a truncation, especially in speech or writing), and *elliptical* (the adjectival form of both ideas).

Our language has thousands of examples of this. However, not all words follow this comfortable domestic trend. Some are so ungainly in shape or sound that they are ill-adapted to the rules which generally govern the relationship between the various parts of speech. *Reductio ad absurdum* is a useful expression, but it is incapable of being modified into an adjective or an adverb, let alone a verb. Where grammatical flexibility is needed, the only option is to use *apagoge, apagogical, apagogically*. Derived from the Greek, it has exactly the same meaning as the Latin.

Generally speaking, words borrowed from other languages do not take variant forms. Words like *Schadenfreude, raison d'etre, hoi polloi, glasnost,* and *perestroika* do not readily lend themselves to variations in English. However, as some loan-words become naturalised, they spawn offspring, generally to the despair of the purists. So, *liaison* was, until recently, considered a foreign word and treated with the courtesy reserved for visitors. But it has stayed on, and is now treated familiarly as a verb: *liaise*. A similar fate has met *ballet* (adjective: *balletic*); *brusque* (noun: *brusqueness*); *charlatan* (parallel noun: *charlatanism*); *chauffeur* (used also as a *verb*); *clique* (adjective: *cliquy*); *elite* (adjective, noun, and parallel noun: *elitism*); *prestige* (noun and adjective, and parallel adjective: *prestigious*), and so on. It is interesting to consider that all of these French words were treated by Fowler as truly foreign words in the first edition of *Modern English Usage*.

Compound words are difficult to transmute from one form to another. *Lighthouse* does not readily turn into a verb or adjective; *bookcase* likewise. *Showcase*, on the other hand, is used as noun and verb (courtesy of television), but does not yet boast an adjective or adverb form.

Some words have been conjured into existence because their form suggests that they are already a member of a family.

This process — backformation — is a prolific source of new words. So the adjective *grovelling* existed, and its form suggested that it was the present participle of an imagined verb, *grovel*. *Grovel* came to be used as a verb and later produced a noun with the same form. An identical process accounts for *ablute* from *ablution*; *automate* from *automation*; *choreograph* and *choreographer* from *choreography*; *co-ordinate* and *co-ordinator* from *co-ordination*; *emote* from *emotion*; *extradite* from *extradition*, and so on. Thus the apparent child begets the imagined parent.

But some words are just themselves, all alone, admitting no variant forms and used only in a single context. These orphans have lived much longer than their relatives whose remains may be found in large dictionaries. *Offing* is an example. The *offing* now is only encountered in the phrase *in the offing*, meaning that the thing referred to is imminent. The *offing* is 'the part of the visible sea distant from the shore or beyond the anchoring ground'. A boat lying at anchor to await a favourable tide before entering the harbour is *in the offing*. William Dampier said in 1703, 'By Nine a Clock at Night we had got a pretty good Offin', — that is, a pretty good resting point some distance from the shore.

Another orphan is *fell*, now used only in expressions of the type *one fell blow*; *one fell swoop*. It is unrelated to the verb *fall*, and unrelated to the verb *fell* (to cause to fall). A *fell blow* is a cruel blow. It derives from the Latin *fello-*: fierce, cruel, savage. *Fell* meant cruel, harsh, destructive, or spirited, doughty. It has more vigorous relatives: *felon* also derives from *fello-*. Its living relatives include *feloness*, *felony*, *felonry*, and *felonious*.

Figment is confined to a corner of the workhouse where its only companion is *the imagination*. Its original sense is *something fashioned or made*. It comes from the Latin *fingere*: to form or mould, which is also the root of *feign*, *fiction*, and *figure*. While each of these has its own family and is often seen out in company, *figment* has not flourished. It is an invention of the mind, and it is perfectly sensible to refer to someone's perjurious story as a *figment of the mind*, a *figment of desperation*, a *figment of the imagination*, or simply a *figment*.

Another orphan, whose parentage is not obvious, is *het*, as in *het up*. If a plaintiff knocks back a generous offer at the start of a difficult and dubious case, their counsel is likely to get *het up*. Although it has the appearance of a dialect word, it is the participial adjective from *heat*, built on the pattern *feed–fed*, *lead–led*. So it simply means *heated up*. It is rarely enough heard, and then only with reference to a person's emotional temperature. I heard it often as a child: generally, it was directed at me.

We use diminutives with children without thinking. The commonest suffix which implies smallness or youth is *–let*. *Booklet*, *piglet*, and *droplet* are obvious examples; *bracelet* is less obvious, since the stem *bracel* is now obsolete. *Farmlet* and *leaflet* are common words constructed on the same lines. Much less familiar, but no less legitimate, are *fanglet* (small fang), *doglet*, *froglet*, *goslet* (small goose), *sharklet* (small shark), and *squirelet* (small squire).

Interestingly, every branch of the nobility has its corresponding diminutive. It must have been hard, as a member of the aristocracy, to be disparaged as a *dukelet* or *kinglet*. So Florio said in Montaigne (1603) 'So many petty-kings, and petty-petty kinglets have we now adayes'. The most unkindest cut.

(Incidentally, we use *orphan* nowadays to signify a person who, as Lady Bracknell would have it, has been so careless as to lose both parents. But originally an *orphan* meant a person who has lost one or both parents.)

MISTAKEN MEANINGS

———◆———

'When *I* use a word,' Humpty Dumpty said in a rather scornful tone, 'it means just what I choose it to mean — neither more nor less.'
(*Through the Looking-Glass*, chapter 6).

This notion works not only for Humpty Dumpty, but for all mankind. Most words begin life with a meaning that is clear, well-defined, and demonstrable. Some are eventually mis-read, misunderstood, or misprinted, and take on a new life and meaning that bears no relation to their origins. Two distinct branches of this phenomenon can be identified.

The first comprises words that have been distorted by some accident and have adopted either a new form or a new meaning (or both). *Helpmeet* is one example. It is the product of a wrong hyphen in Genesis 2:18, in which God decides to 'make an help meet for him' (Adam). *Meet*, in the context, means 'suitable'. In some translations, it is written 'an help

131

answering to him'. An inadvertent seventeenth-century hyphen produced *help-meet*, and a new word was assumed and invested with meaning. An accident of typesetting, it is etymological nonsense, but it endures.

Also from the Bible comes *scapegoat*. It is a genuine word, but its meaning has never accorded with the sense in which it was coined. It is exclusively used in its spurious sense. In Leviticus 16:8 Aaron offers the Lord two goats. He casts lots on them, one for the Lord and the other for a scape-goat (that is, a goat to escape, to be freed). The Lord's goat is killed (verse 15) and the scape-goat is released into the wilderness (verse 10). So, originally it was the scapegoat which survived; now it is otherwise.

Psychological moment is an example of a related process. We adopted it (mistakenly) to mean a *decisive instant, a critical time*. We then eroded it until the received meaning is now 'the nick of time'. All quite mistaken. In 1871, during the Franco-Prussian war, the Prussian forces were poised to bombard Paris. The Kreuz newspaper referred to the proposed bombardment, and to *das psychologische Moment* of that bombardment.

German grammar recognises three genders. 'Der Moment' (masculine) means 'moment' or 'second'. 'Das Moment' (neuter) means 'momentum'. So, *das psychologische Moment* means 'psychological momentum' — the likely effect the bombardment would have on French morale.

Appropriately enough, we get the expression via the French '*moment psychologique*'. Understandably, the French use it as meaning 'the moment in which the mind is in actual expectation of something that is to happen'. So it must have been in 1871. By this accidental path we got an expression that does not mean what it should, but serves a useful purpose nonetheless.

Tweed comes from a misprint. The cloth was called *tweel* (Scottish dialect for *twill*). In 1831, a Scottish cloth merchant's catalogue misprinted it as *tweed*. By chance, the principal cloth-weaving area of Scotland is in the region of the River Tweed. By an association of ideas, the misprint stuck. Humpty Dumpty would have been proud.

Syllabus is another product of a misprint. In Cicero's letters to Atticus, he refers to *sittubas*, which is the accusative plural form of *sittuba*, a title slip or label that identifies the contents of a manuscript. In a 1470 edition of Cicero, it was misprinted as *syllabus*. The altered form took root, and the meaning drifted from its origins. Although it is a Greek plural, it looks like a Latin singular; so it is now used in the singular and given a Latin plural: *syllabi*. This has the double disadvantage of being both ugly and misconceived. It is too late to insist that syllabus is not singular; but syllabuses is to be preferred for the plural.

Although it is irrelevant to the theme of this essay, plurals of imported words bring out the best and worst in English speakers. *Octopus* is often heard in the plural as *octopi* — this, presumably, as a display of classical erudition. But *octopus* is not Latin; it is Greek ('eight foot'). The Greek plural is *octopodes* (as in *antipodes*, 'other feet', meaning the opposite side). Since we have adopted the word so completely, we should give it an English plural: *octopuses*.

The second branch of the phenomenon is the ghost word. These rare creatures haunt dictionaries for a time; occasionally they escape into the real world. They differ from *mumpsimus* only in that they are created by lexicographers, and when they are exposed they generally fade away.

Dord was, for a time, defined in Webster (1934) as meaning 'density in physics or chemistry'. It was entirely wrong: a typesetter had misread 'D or d, density in physics or chemistry'. It is seen no more.

Howl was for a time picked up in dictionaries as a Scottish spelling of *hovel*. That was almost right, but not quite. The dialect word is *howf* or *howff* — defined by the *OED2* as 'a place of resort, a haunt, a resort'. (Curious that it should be a haunt: it gave rise to a ghost word, and is also the name of the burial ground at Dundee). *Howf* was thus understood as a place where people lived, and appeared to be related to hovel. The English lexicographers' traditional disdain for the Scots combined with a typesetting error, and *howl* roamed the dictionaries for a time as a crude dwelling-house.

Samuel Johnson enlivened his many triumphs with some spectacular blunders. Asked once why he had defined *pastern* as the 'knee of a horse', he replied 'Ignorance, madam, pure ignorance'. And for his attitude to the Scots, see his definition of *oats*. He is the father of a ghost word: *foupe*. His *Dictionary* describes it as follows:

> to FOUPE v.a. To drive with a sudden impetuosity. A word out of use.

'We pronounce, by the concession of strangers, as smoothly and moderately as any of the northern nations, who foupe their words out of the throat with fat and full spirits.' – Camden.

Well, he was partly right — it was certainly out of use. But it had never been in use. The word as printed in Camden was *soupe*. (With the archaic long form of *s*, the mistake was easily made.) It is a dialect word with a meaning akin to *swoop*. Dr Todd's edition of Johnson (1818) spotted the error and left it there, but pointed it out. The *OED2* also records it. (It does not record *Dord*, but that was an American mistake.) It identifies it as an error for *soupe*. Being thus exposed as a ghost, but recorded anyway, makes *foupe* a shadow of a ghost: unique so far as I know.

Most ghost words are ephemeral; but during its brief existence in Johnson's London, *foupe* was exported to Barbados. Presumably it went there as part of sailors' cant. However that may be, it came into use there, meaning the rollicking copulation of animals (not humans). It is the sort of word politely castigated by dictionaries as *(vulg.)* or *(not in polite use)*. It is seen in the ad hoc social comments of graffiti artists and other nostalgic philologists, 200 years after its chimerical parent faded away in England. If Barbadians compile a dictionary of their language, *foupe* will presumably materialise there, and will join *syllabus* as a ghost legitimised at last.

NAUGHTY WORDS

◆

Samuel Johnson defined *fart* as meaning *to break wind behind*. He illustrated the usage with a quotation from Swift:

> As when we do a gun discharge,
> Although the bore be ne'er so large,
> Before the flames from muzzle burst,
> Just at the breech it flashes first;
> So from my Lord his passions broke,
> He *farted* first, and then he spoke.

I have not been able to find out who was the object of Swift's attention. It was probably Lord Chesterfield, who was much despised by Johnson. Johnson described Chesterfield's letters to his son as '…*teaching the morals of a whore and the manners of a dancing-master*'. However that may be, it is apparent that *fart* was not treated in the eighteenth century with the reserve now accorded it. The *OED2* says *fart* is 'not now in decent use', which is about a 6 on the lexicographer's Richter scale of naughtiness. Compare:

damn: no caution, but best not said to a duchess or in court (say 2 on the Richter scale);

bum, turd: 'not in polite use' (say 3);

wank: 'slang' (4);

bugger: 'low language' (5);

bloody: 'foul language' (7, but in Australian usage it is about a 3);

arse: noted as obsolete in polite use, which puts it with *bum* (appropriate anatomically, but in my view it rates a 5); and

fuck and *cunt*: 'for centuries, and still by the great majority, regarded as a taboo-word; until recent times not often recorded in print but frequent in coarse speech' (off the scale)

Oddly, there is not much naughty language available above 6 unless you want to go off the scale.

Of course, these ratings are my own invention and highly subjective, although I doubt there would be much disagreement about the ranking. But the ranking was not always so. *Fart* was more or less in polite use until the eighteenth century. Chaucer used *fart* freely, and the English translations of Aristophanes have him also using it frequently.

Florio's *Dictionary* of 1598 defines a *fizzle* as 'a close farte'. (*OED2* defines *fizzle*, without qualification about its social standing, as 'the action of breaking wind quietly'.) The entry in Florio's *Dictionary* suggests that *fart(e)* was itself regarded as standard English at the time. The same inference is supported by the publication in 1722 of a pamphlet entitled *The Benefit of Farting Explained.* By contrast, *OED2* gives as one meaning of *raspberry* 'a breaking of wind or "fart"'. The use of inverted commas clearly signals that the word is used with diffidence.

According to John Aubrey's *Brief Lives*, Edward de Vere, the 17th Earl of Oxford, accidentally broke wind 'while making low obeisance' to Queen Elizabeth I. He exiled himself for seven years, and when he returned and again met the Queen she said 'My Lord, I had forgotten the fart'. So far as I can find, Shakespeare did not use *fart*: too regal, perhaps. Coming to the present time, Elizabeth II is unlikely to use the word, although the same cannot be said of Princess Anne.

Nowadays, *fart* as a word is heard about as often as the thing it describes. As is the case with many other naughty words, the thing it describes is known to all, done by most, but spoken by few.

Shit and *turd* are words with similar meanings and similar histories. They are both old Saxon words, found in written English from the earliest times. Bailey's dictionary of 1742 and Johnson's of 1755 give definitions of *turd*, with no suggestion that it is a word to be avoided. Bailey also has *shite*: 'to ease nature; to discharge the belly', but Johnson does not. Both words were used liberally by Chaucer. Shakespeare uses *turd* once only (*Merry Wives of Windsor*, Act 3 scene iii), in a pun for *third*. He does not say *shit*, preferring *dung* and *ordure*.

Just as the fortunes of these naughty words have fluctuated, so have the fortunes of *naughty* itself. Originally, *naughty* meant 'having nothing, needy', from *naught/nought*. Soon, the need was principally one of virtue: to be naughty was to be morally bankrupt. So in the King James version of the Bible:

Proverbs 17:4 A wicked doer giveth heed to false lips; [and] a liar giveth ear to a *naughty* tongue.

It also applied to inanimate things which lacked the qualities for which they were otherwise valued:

Jeremiah 24:2 One basket [had] very good figs, [even] like the figs [that are] first ripe: and the other basket [had] very *naughty figs*, which could not be eaten, they were so bad.

At about the same time, Shakespeare often used *naughty*, and invariably to convey real wickedness, as the context shows. In *King Lear*, the unlovable Regan, whose treachery has been discovered by Gloucester, is addressed by him thus:

Naughty lady,
These hairs which thou dost ravish from my chin
Will quicken, and accuse thee. I am your host.
With robber's hands my hospitable favours
You should not ruffle thus. What will you do?

(The question is rhetorical, but an answer is swift: Regan's husband tears out Gloucester's eyes).

In 1752, Nathaniel Bailey's dictionary defined *naughty* as 'wicked, lewd'. Johnson (1755) defined it as 'bad, wicked, corrupt', but noted that it was 'now seldom used but in ludicrous censure'. By degrees, *naughty* came to be the mildest rebuke. So, in *Wuthering Heights* (1847): 'I attempted to persuade him of the *naughtiness* of showing reluctance to meet his father ...'

At least until the end of the sixteenth century, then, it was probably safer to call a person a *fart* or a *turd* than to suggest they were *naughty*.

NEW WORDS

———◆———

The urge to invent words is almost as powerful as the language instinct itself. Children freely invent words; lovers develop a private language; and most families have a few invented words of their own.

Shakespeare famously invented a huge number of words, or pressed existing words into service with an altered meaning. Advertisers invent and distort words, albeit with enough restraint to avoid alienating their audience. New occupations and altered social circumstances generate a vocabulary to deal with novel ideas and phenomena associated with them.

Here are some new words which are gaining currency, especially in the USA:

404 (noun). an obstacle or barrier, preventing attainment of a goal. It derives from the error message returned on the internet if a specified file cannot be found at a site.

The message reads: '404 file not found'. It is a common irritation, which has passed naturally into the everyday speech of computer nerds.

411 (noun): information or informative details, usually about a planned event or activity. Sometimes said as 4-1-1. It derives from the fact that, in the USA, 411 is widely reserved as the telephone number for information lines. An equivalent construction in Australia is 0055, as an oblique reference to something sordid or salacious, from the fact that phone-sex services use the 0055 phone block *'He had a night of 0055'*.

BFE (adj.): very far away (Beyond Fucking Egypt).

Blamestorming: a group discussion, the purpose of which is to determine whose fault caused the problem or disaster that now has to be fixed or paid for. Anyone who ever lost expensive litigation will understand it. Blamestorming sessions may have to be conducted by sub-groups: solicitors and associates, to blame the articled clerks or barristers; the lawyers collectively, to blame the witnesses; the clients and their consultants, to blame the lawyers; and so on.

Chainsaw Consultant: an external consultant whose job is to reduce the size of the workforce brutally, leaving the board and management blameless.

Cube Farm: a office where the partitioning reaches just above head-height, dividing the open area into a series of open cubicles.

Ego Surfing: the practice of scanning the Net and searching electronic databases looking for references to one's own name. Also called 'self-Googling'.

Email: electronic mail. The most-used facet of computer networks including, notably, the internet.

Fashionista: a person fanatically devoted to the extremes of high-fashion.

Fun (used as an adjective) e.g: 'We had a fun time'; 'She has a fun job'.

Further-fetched: beyond far-fetched.

Going Postal: the reaction of a person with a low stress-threshold who is pushed beyond endurance by relatively trivial events, and goes crazy; a reference to postal employees who have snapped and gone on shooting rampages. The character Newman, in the Seinfeld show, was a stereotype of such a character.

Keyboard Plaque: the disgusting film of dark-grey material on a computer keyboard.

K-Mart express: a girl of easy virtue and limited discernment.

Losingest: in last place, worst off, lagging behind the rest. (First spotted in the *Wall Street Journal* in 1989, when the former high-flyers of Wall Street were among the losingest of the corporate fall-outs).

Mallrats: groups of feral children, generally dressed in oversized trousers, big-name sports shoes, and reversed baseball caps, who hang around shopping malls. Where possible, they travel by skateboard.

McJob: a service job, with low pay and limited prospects; a horizontal career path for losers.

Midair Passenger Exchange: air-traffic control

euphemism for a collision between two aircraft. It is followed by aluminium rain.

Mouse potato: computer nerd.

Ohnosecond: the instant during which you realise that you have made a catastrophic, irreversible mistake.

Percussive maintenance: the art of hitting an electronic device to make it function.

Prairie dogging: the result of making a loud noise in a cube farm: co-workers stand up and peer over the partitions to see what is going on.

Rubber-chicken circuit: the succession of obligatory lunches and dinners attended by politicians and professional fund-raisers.

Seagull manager: a manager who flies in, makes a lot of noise, shits on everything, and then flies out again.

Shopgrifting: obtaining short-term use of an item by buying it on credit and returning it within the warranty period for a refund.

Snail mail: standard mail, as opposed to email.

Spam: sending the same email message to huge numbers of email addresses. Junk email.

Swiped out: the condition of a credit card which has become electronically unreadable.

Umfriend: an undeclared sexual partner. 'This is Robin, my ... um ... friend ...'

Way: (used as an adjective) very, extremely: 'The party was way fun'; 'He is way cool'

Web rage: road rage on the information superhighway; the result of slow internet access speeds turning the

Infobahn into the World Wide Wait.

Whatever: (as absolute pronoun) Expression of indifference or equanimity when faced with various possibilities *Q*: 'Would you prefer tea or coffee? *A*: 'Whatever'; (as verb) to induce a sensation of indifference; to leave an indelible blank in the mind 'That person whatevers me'.

Some of these expressions have caught on widely, and are likely to survive (*email, snail mail, spam, McJob, whatever, postal*). In fact, it is hard to believe that *spam* and *email* are such recent expressions. Others deserve to survive (such as *web rage, mouse potato, percussive maintenance, seagull manager, umfriend, swiped out*). The rest are likely to fade away as fast as they arose. But, with English, who can tell?

NICE DISTINCTIONS

———◆———

Of all the words in the English language, few have had more varied careers than *nice*. Its meaning has altered more often than that of most other words, and it has always borne several different meanings simultaneously. It was once a verbal chameleon, whose instability might have threatened its survival; it is now much overworked, and has sunk to the verbal equivalent of a food extender, or flavouring 101.

Currently, *nice* has two main meanings. The more common is *agreeable* (generally in a somewhat diluted sense); the other is *fine, narrow, subtle,* as in a *nice question*, a *nice distinction.*

Nice originally meant *stupid.* It derives from the Latin *nescius*, meaning ignorant. It is thus closely related to *nescient* (ignorant) and *nescience* (lack of knowledge, ignorance). Its progress from there to its two current meanings is a matter of conjecture. But the course of its progress can be charted by noting the 15 principal definitions given it in the *OED2*, with

the dates of the earliest and latest quotations supplied by the
OED2 as illustrating those meanings:

1 foolish, stupid, senseless (1290 to 1560);

2 wanton, loose-mannered, lascivious (1325 to 1606); (of
dress) extravagant, flaunting (1430 to1540); very trim,
elegant or smart (1483 to 1540);

3 strange, rare, uncommon (1430 to 1555);

4 slothful, lazy, indolent (1440 to 1604); effeminate,
unmanly (1573 to 1681); tender, delicate (1562 to 1710);
over-refined, luxurious (1621 to 1720);

5 coy, shy, affectedly modest (1400 to 1634); reluctant,
unwilling (1560 to 1676);

6 *to make it* **nice** to display reserve or reluctance; to make a
scruple (1530 to 1677);

7 fastidious, dainty, difficult to please in matters of food or
cleanliness; refined (1551 to 1782); particular, precise,
strict (1584 to 1861); fastidious in matters of literary taste
(1628 to 1770); precise or strict in matters of reputation
or conduct; punctilious, scrupulous, sensitive (1647 to
1887); refined, cultured (1603 to 1874);

8 requiring or involving great precision, accuracy or
minuteness (1513 to 1840);

9 not obvious or readily apprehended; difficult to decide
(1513 to 1885); minute, subtle (1561 to 1870); precise,
exact, fine (1710 to 1867);

10 slender, thin (1590 to 1604); unimportant, trivial (1592 to
1601);

11 critical, doubtful, full of danger or uncertainty (1596 to

1682); delicate, needing tactful handling (1617to 1777);

12 entering minutely into detail, attentive, close (1589 to 1864); (of the senses) able to distinguish or discriminate in a high degree (1586 to 1873); (of judgment) finely discriminative (1597 to 1845); delicate or skilful in manipulation (1711 to 1807);

13 minutely or carefully accurate (1599 to 1875);

14 (of food) dainty, appetizing (especially of a cup of tea!) (1712 to 1974); and

15 agreeable, a source of pleasure or satisfaction (1796 to 1975).

It is interesting to note how many senses of the word were current in Shakespeare's time. So far as we know, his plays were written between 1592 and 1605. During that time, quotations from the *OED2* suggest that *nice* was being used in all of the meanings set out above other than 1, 3, 14, and 15. According to the quotations given by the *OED2*, Shakespeare used the word in each of senses 2, 6, 10, 11, and 13.

Perhaps because the word was such a chameleon during the time he was writing, Shakespeare used it sparingly. In total, he used *nice* in twenty-four of his 42 plays, where it appears only 33 times. This is no mean feat, since it might be thought difficult to use a word at all which simultaneously meant *wanton*, *lascivious*, *scrupulous*, *trivial*, and *minutely accurate*. By comparison, Wilde used *nice* 15 times in *A Woman of No Importance*. That play was written in 1893, by which time the meaning of *nice* had stabilised to the two which are currently understood, and context makes the intended meaning quite plain. In this simple comparison, there is a point to be made in the argument between the conservatives and the language libertarians.

In that happy group which dabbles in language, one of the main philosophical divisions concerns tolerance of change. The conservatives and the libertarians wage war with lexicographers and each other about whether words should be allowed to change meaning, and whether dictionaries should dignify ignorant change by recording it. H.W. Fowler was the most vocal of conservatives. He watched the battle between ignorant usage and semantic purity, constantly tending the wounds of the injured, and lighting candles for the victims. The *Macquarie Dictionary* (produced by Macquarie University in Australia) is sometimes attacked as a haven for the libertarians, as it notes without censure the most ignorant misuse alongside the original meaning. See, for example, its note in the third edition under the entry for *fulsome*: 'the shift in meaning of this word from "offensive to good taste" to "lavish, unstinted" offends some writers but seems to have gained acceptance with the majority'. Nicely put.

Shakespeare's relatively sparing use of *nice* illustrates the point that a word whose meaning is ambiguous is likely to be shunned by those who would make their meaning clear. This is probably the most powerful argument of the language conservatives: if change is tolerated without restraint or censure, the stock of useful words is diminished. As words are used in a sense not previously recognised, it becomes more difficult to use the word with any confidence that your meaning will be received intact. Despite the Macquarie's comforting verdict, I would hesitate to use *fulsome* for any purpose, except to be ironic or mischievous; likewise *vagary*, which is now often used to mean *vagueness*; and *disinterested*, which is wrongly used to mean *uninterested*. There are many other words that cannot now be used with confidence, because it is likely that their meaning will be confused with that of another because of repeated misuse. Examples are *alternate* (thought to mean *alternative*); *emotive* (thought to mean *emotional*); *decimate* (thought to mean *destroy*); *congenial* (thought to mean *genial*); *exponential* (thought to mean *rapid*); *dimension* thought to mean size, scale, or some other ill-defined characteristic); and *exotic* (thought to mean anything unusual).

The *Macquarie Dictionary* is an admirable record of the current state of Australian English. Whether you find the current state of the language satisfactory or not is a matter of taste; whether you consider the Macquarie's approach to lexicography right or not is likewise a matter of taste. Whether you venture an opinion about these things in public depends on your willingness to provoke others to heated argument. If anyone asks your opinion of the Macquarie, it is quite safe to say 'nice work' (if they don't get it).

Have a nice day.

OBSCENE WORDS

———◆———

In late 1996, the Court of Appeal in New South Wales passed judgement upon the use of the word *fuck* by a policeman to a female subordinate. Although the decision turned on other points, a question arose whether it constitutes offensive behaviour to use the word, and its variants, in a police station. The decision in *Commissioner of Police* v *Anderson* (CA NSW unrep 21 October 1996) thus provides an interesting starting point for a bit of harmless etymology.

The case was an application to review a decision of the Police Tribunal. It had found that Anderson had 'failed to show respect for his subordinates', but it dismissed a charge that he had 'used offensive language in a public place'. The commissioner sought to review the dismissal, saying that he had not had a proper opportunity to prove that the Blacktown Police Station was a 'public place'.

The Court of Appeal said the decision was not reviewable on that ground. Meagher JA went on to say that in any event the words spoken did not amount to offensive language in the circumstances.

The words complained of were spoken to a female officer, Constable Cowin. They included the following passages of limpid prose:

> Constable, get fucking over here … why aren't these fucking messages on the fucking pad … I don't fucking care, I want them on the fucking pad …

The charges also alleged that Anderson used the word *cunt*, although not to Constable Cowin.

The decision of all three members of the court was that the commissioner had had a proper opportunity to prove that the police station was a public place, so it dismissed the application.

Meagher JA said in addition that the words spoken were not offensive. He said:

> Undoubtedly, the behaviour of (Anderson) was unchivalrous and unbecoming of the office he occupies. This is, however, a long way from … being offensive in any sense.
>
> The evidence discloses that Sergeant Anderson habitually used the word 'fuck' or its derivatives; that everyone else did also; that Constable Cowin herself did so regularly. It was, so a witness said, part of what oxymoronically is called 'police culture'. Likewise, the word 'cunt' (is) used from time to time, although Sergeant

Anderson never used this word to Constable Cowin. There was no evidence that persons in the public area were ever offended, nor that the public area was frequented by gentle old ladies or convent schoolgirls. Bearing in mind that we are living in a post-Chatterley, post-Wolfenden age, taking into account all circumstances, and judging the matter from the point of view of reasonable contemporary standards, I cannot believe that Sergeant Anderson's language was legally 'offensive'.

Fuck is an interesting word, linguistically speaking. It has the virtues of brevity, adaptability, expressiveness, and is understood universally. It has a huge number of synonyms, ranging from coy euphemisms to acceptable jocular equivalents to coarse vulgarities.

Oddly, it has very few polite equivalents. Strictly speaking, there is no single English word in current use that bears the same primary meaning. It may be thought that *copulate* is an exact synonym for the verb *to fuck*, but *copulate* has a broader meaning: 'To couple, conjoin, link together; to become conjoined or united'. In its sexual meaning, it is primarily confined to zoology.

Fornicate is the second contender; but it is, strictly, confined to sexual intercourse between a man and an unmarried woman.

According to the second edition of the *Oxford English Dictionary*, the only verb which has as its only meaning 'engage in sexual intercourse' is *subagitate*. However, that word has not been recorded in use since 1693. Not until now, that is.

In order to refer to the activity which *fuck* describes, it is necessary to engage in circumlocution or periphrasis. Thus we get *make love to; sleep with; engage in sexual relations with*, etc.

Along with *cunt, fuck* was excluded from dictionaries and almost all writing from the end of the eighteenth century until the Lady Chatterley trial in 1960, when both words were welcomed back from the Siberian gulags of condemned words. Not without difficulty, it has since made its way onto stage and screen. It must be said that an activity which is so popular and widespread has been poorly served by polite language.

It was not always so. *Fuck* is recorded as being used in more-or-less respectable literature as early as 1500, and it is found in Florio's Italian-English dictionary (1598).

It is interesting to reflect on the social process which results in a (nearly) universal activity having no convenient and polite verbal tag to denote it: the activity becomes very inconvenient to discuss, and so it is not discussed, at least in Polite Society. Suppose a group of intelligent, decent, and literate people wish to discuss sex. Instead of using *fuck* as verb and noun, they must resort to *have sexual intercourse with* (verb); and *an act of sexual intercourse* (noun). Instead of the participial use *fucking*, they must say *having sexual intercourse*, and likewise for the verbal noun form *fucking*. And even these inelegancies involve a circumlocution, since *intercourse* is a word of wider application.

George Orwell wrote of the use of language to control

thought (see especially his treatise on Newspeak in *Nineteen Eighty Four*). The same process has made talk about sex so difficult if social conventions are to be observed. Not surprisingly, a huge number of slang and colloquial words have sprung up to liberate thought and language in the middle ground between polite speech and the taboo-word.

Although the following words all describe the same thing, they have won acceptance, if not in the salon, at least in the outer-rooms of polite society: *play mothers and fathers, go upstairs, make babies, get one's jollies, play hide the sausage, get into one's pants, have a tumble.* And then there are the earthier monosyllabic inventions: *stuff, screw, pork, poke, bang, bonk, root, hump.* Note that these can be used both as verb and noun. Interestingly, it is easy to see that some of these synonyms are more acceptable than others, but all are more accepted than *fuck.* Generally, the more humorous the construction, the more acceptable it is.

There are many jocular noun constructions which also provide the same meaning, and range in acceptability, although none of them has the versatility of their one-word equivalents: *Ugandan affairs, country matters, parallel parking, horizontal folk-dancing, you know what, indoor sledging, knee-trembler.* Again, as the allusion retreats from sex and approaches humour, it becomes more acceptable.

Then there is swive: 'swive, v. Obs or arch:

1. trans. To have sexual connexion with, copulate with (a female)
2. intr. To copulate...

I had always believed, before I checked it, that *swive* was a slang word. In fact, it is a sturdy Old English word, related to the Old High German *sweib* (meaning sweep or swing). But for the fact that (apparently) its primary meaning is not gender neutral, it deserves to be ranked alongside *subagitate*.

Chaucer used it in *The Miller's Tale*, *The Reeve's Tale*, and also in *The Manciple's Tale*:

> For all your watching, bleared is your bright eye
> By one of small repute, as well is known,
> Not worth, when I compare it with your own,
> The value of a gnat, as I may thrive.
> For on your bed your wife I saw him swive.

Chaucer's use of the word may not be enough to ensure its respectability. On balance, it may still be advisable to prefer *subagitate* in genteel company, where clarity of meaning is traditionally subordinated to elegance. But *swive* is justifiable on historical grounds.

In April 1914, Mrs Patrick Campbell created a sensation in London by uttering the word *bloody* on the stage, in the first performance of *Pygmalion*. That word had been banned from books and stage since the middle of the eighteenth century. Before then it had been accepted in polite use, but had gradually fallen into disgrace. Since George Bernard Shaw took the daring step of writing it into *Pygmalion*, it has returned to acceptable use. Only in the most proper circles would it raise eyebrows now. Its only use (relevantly) is as an intensifier.

Looked at solely as a lexical unit, *fuck* is a very good, sturdy, versatile, and descriptive word. If our social masters could reconcile themselves to the idea that sex is a legitimate part of human existence and is here to stay, it may be that *fuck* will eventually be accepted in polite use.

ODD CONNECTIONS #1

———◆———

S ome words openly display their pedigree: they convey a fairly obvious hint of their own origins. This is especially so when they are derived directly from Latin or Greek, or indirectly from Latin by way of French. They may change their form over time, but the meaning remains more or less constant from the progenitor to the progeny.

Other words are much more obliquely connected to their origins, and turn out to be connected to other, apparently unrelated, words. Take *pedigree*, for example. It is very far from obvious that it is etymologically derived from the crane's foot. In Middle French *pié* (*pied*) *de grue* is the *foot of the crane*. In early manuscripts, lines of descent were so drawn as to suggest the footprint of a crane, and the resemblance provided a metaphor for the relations depicted in the diagram. Introduced into English in the fifteenth century, the word was originally spelled *pee-de-grew*, *pedegru*, or *pedicru*. Johnson's first edition attributed the origins of the word as *pere* + *degré*, and attributed this to Skinner. In the fourth edition, Johnson still relies on Skinner, but has it as *per* + *degré*.

Stephen Skinner's *Etymologicon Linguae Anglicanae* (1671) displayed a distinct bias for finding a classical origin for every English word. This was consonant with the thinking of seventeenth- and eighteenth-century English grammarians, who sought to devise a coherent set of rules for English modelled on a 'perfect language'. Latin was perceived as logical and stable. It was highly logical, especially by comparison with the chaos of seventeenth-century English. Certainly it was stable, since it had been dead for centuries. This neo-classical bias led to many oddities. Not the least was the fact that Skinner's dictionary — a dictionary of English etymology, written by an Englishmen for English speakers — was written in Latin. Another, more enduring, oddity was the rule that an infinitive could not be split.

To boldly go breaches the injunction against splitting infinitives. It has become one of the world's famous split infinitives, often repeated or parodied, after its use in the title scenes of *Star Trek*. However, it has no special advantage of emphasis or clarity over *to go boldly*. By contrast, *to cheerfully sing again* conveys clearly what is otherwise ambiguous in *to sing cheerfully again*: in adhering to the rule, the second statement leaves the hearer uncertain whether the cheerfulness qualifies the method of singing or the fact of doing it again.

There is an odd thing about the English horror of split infinitives. It is based on the observation that Latin infinitives *could not* be split, with the conclusion that English infinitives *must not* be split. Latin infinitives could not split because they were in the form of a single word such as *amare*: to love; *habere*: to have: and *cantare*: to sing, etc. In consequence of the early grammarians' sturdy adherence to the conventions of Latin, we daily wrestle with tensions created by the rule.

It is hard to imagine that the traditional measure of a diamond's weight is in any way connected to the rhinoceros, yet it is. The link is the ancient Greek word *keras*: a horn, and *keratos:* a little horn. The rhinoceros' name means literally *nose-horn*. The fruit of the carob tree has the form of a small horn, and was called *keratos* by the ancient Greeks. It was used as a measure of small weight. After passing through various forms, the spelling stabilised as *carat*, disguising the link to the horn and the carob tree. As a measure of weight, the *carat* was $1/24$ of the golden solidus of Constantine, which was $1/6$ of an ounce.

The rhinoceros horn, incidentally, is made of hair. That does not break the etymological link, since the structural protein of hair (and of hoof, nails, and feathers) is *keratin*, named after the seed of the carob tree.

The connection between the Fates and the fairies is not obvious. Originally, *fairy (faerie, fayre)* was the land or home of the fays. It was a collective noun for a number of fays. A *fay* was what we would now call a fairy. The word came into English from French *fée*, which comes from old French *faie*, derived in turn from Latin *fata*, the Fates. The use of *fairy* to refer to a singular instance of the breed arose as early as the fifteenthth century, but *fay* continued in parallel use until the mid-nineteenth century. Johnson defines *fay* as 'a fairy, an elf', and defines *fairy* as: 'A kind of fabled being supposed to appear in a diminutive human form, and to dance in the meadows, and reward cleanliness in houses; an elf; a fay …'

The most famous fay of English mythology is *Morgane le Fay* of the Arthurian legend. She was King Arthur's sister, and was said to have learned her skills as healer and enchantress from Merlin. When Arthur was mortally wounded in battle, it was Morgane le Fay who carried him in a barge to the Island of Avalon where (according to your preference) he died or she healed him.

In various parts of the Mediterranean Sea, a mirage is sometimes seen which was imagined to be the magical sister of King Arthur. The mirage is most often seen in the Straits of Messina, where Italian sailors call her *Fata Morgana*. In Italian, the direct connection between the fairies and the Fates is explicit. The word was adopted back into English. So Melville says in *Moby Dick*: 'Soon they through dim, bewildering mediums saw her sidelong fading phantom, as in the gaseous *Fata Morgana* …'

The expression has been broadened in English, although not very often used, as meaning any mirage. Thus Carlyle wrote that Coleridge: 'preferred to create logical *fatamorganas* for himself on this hither side.'

Another group of words whose connectedness is not apparent is *eager*, *acid*, *acrid*, and *vinegar*. The link is their common Latin root *ac-* meaning sharp, yielding *acer–acrem* sour, pungent, swift, strenuous. This yielded Old French *aigre* (sharp, keen, sour) that is easily recognised in the modern

French *vinaigre* (vinegar), literally *sharp wine*. The word *eager* came to English via Old French. The English spellings of it have included *aygre, aeygre, eigre, eygre, eger,* and *egar*.

Applied to human character, *eager* originally meant strenuous, ardent, or impetuous; and applied to animals, it meant savage or fierce. Johnson defines it as:

'Struck with desire; ardently wishing; keenly desirous; vehement in desire; hotly longing; Hot of disposition; vehement; ardent; impetuous.'

Its current meaning is weaker.

Another English word currently combines all the previous meanings of *eager*, and that is *keen*. It originally meant bold, brave, learned; then sharp or having an effect on the senses similar to that of a sharp edge, hence pungent, piercing. So an employee may be keen, as can a blade, or a biting wind, or a person's eyesight, or hot chilli pepper. *Keen as mustard* is not a pun on the name of the manufacturer — rather the reverse.

The earliest form of *keen* is found in Old Scandinavian *koni*; it is found in various forms in Middle Dutch *coene* and Old German *koene*, but it is not found outside the Teutonic languages. It is very old: it is recorded as early as 897. Most of its extended or metaphorical senses were recognised by the fourteenth century. Little wonder that the language had so little difficulty adopting *eager* in the fourteenth century and extending its meaning throughout the fifteenth and sixteenth centuries. They were true synonyms originally, but the newcomer *eager* has gradually dwindled in force while *keen* has retained its original edge.

ODD CONNECTIONS #2

Most of our vocabulary comes directly or indirectly from Latin or Greek; but the vocabulary of modern English is far greater than the sum of ancient Latin and Greek vocabularies. The difference is not explained by our borrowings from other languages. The reason English has grown much larger than the sources from which it springs is that a single root word in Latin or Greek will be found to have spawned many offspring in English. This explains the enormous size of the English lexicon: the latest estimate is that English comprises 616,500 words. It also explains why words that may seem quite unrelated, and with widely different meanings, on investigation turn out to be distant cousins.

Consider *exult*: 'to manifest arrogant or scornful delight by speech or behaviour'. Strange to find that it is related to each of the following words: *assail, resile, salient, salacious, salmon, and somersault*. The common ancestor of all these is the Latin *salire*: to jump or leap. *Assail* is defined in *OED2* as 'To leap upon or at, esp. with hostile intent'. To *resile* is to spring back or withdraw. A *salient* is originally something which leaps forward, then something which stands out prominently, especially a piece of land which juts out from its surrounding coastline. Used as an adjective, it signifies something that stands out prominently: in argument, a salient point is a point of great importance or significance.

The connection with *salacious* is less direct: *salire* is the root of *salaci-, salax:* lustful, lecherous, wanton. It was not always connected with sex, although it would be dangerous to use it now if a reference to sex was not intended. In 1661 Feltham wrote '... you have seen how the salacious and devouring Sparrow beat out the harmless Marten from his nest.' And in 1675 Evelyn wrote of 'Pigeons, Poultry and other salacious Corn-fed Birds.' It seems unlikely that the sexual behaviour of sparrows, pigeons, and poultry has altered much since the seventeenth century (although battery hens face a short and abstinent life by comparison with their free-range ancestors). Apparently their *salacity* consisted in jumping for more general purposes. *Jumping* is still used figuratively in sexual slang ('go the jump'), but it is beyond the scope of this essay to explore that interesting byway.

Somersault is more obviously connected to *salire* than is the spawning conduct of salmon which connects them to it. Nature has inflicted on salmon the most awkward instincts when it comes to reproduction: they swim as far as 3000 kilometres to return to the place where they had their origins, and this generally involves a good deal of uphill swimming:

leaping up falls and rapids against all odds and commonsense. The dramatic absurdity of a fish leaping out of the water to fight its way upstream must have been uppermost in the mind of the person who gave the salmon its name.

A related feature of the English language — and one of its torments — is the existence of words that look and sound similar but have meanings which are quite different. Linguistic Darwinism should have weeded out these odd couples long ago — or half of each pair at least — because the confusing similarity of the unlikely partners tends to weaken one or both. But they limp along, the difference between them blurred by misuse, leaving the hearer to gather the intended meaning from the context in which they are deployed.

Examples of this unhappy confusion are exult/exalt, desultory/desolate, enervate/energise, and venal/venial. There are many others.

To *exult*, as noted above, is to manifest arrogant or scornful delight by speech or behaviour. To *exalt* is almost the opposite: it is to raise or set up on high; to lift up, elevate. It comes from the Latin *ex* + *altus*: high. Best not to confuse the two.

Desolate is readily understood. Used as a verb, it involves laying waste, causing utter destruction. Ambrose Bierce, in his *Devil's Dictionary*, defined a *garter* as: 'An elastic band intended to keep a woman from coming out of her stockings and *desolating* the country'; and a *creditor* as 'One of a tribe of savages dwelling beyond the Financial Straits and dreaded for their *desolating* incursions'.

As an adjective it is equally familiar: remember the last winning case you lost; the last sure-thing bet at the race-track; or the spirit of a Collingwood supporter at grand final time. Originally it had the sense of being left entirely alone (from *solus*: alone); hence having the characteristics of a place abandoned and without trees, in a ruinous state; and of a person destitute of joy or comfort.

> Mr. Rochester then turned to the spectators: he looked at
> them with a smile both acrid and desolate.
> (Charlotte Bronte, *Jane Eyre*)

I have frequently heard *desultory* used as if it were a blend of *desolate* and *sultry*, which is a nice idea but wrong. It is another descendent of *salire*, and is more closely related to the leaping salmon and the salacious pigeon than the marauding creditor or the unhappy Rochester. It means jumping or flitting about from one place to another. It is most commonly used qualifying the noun 'conversation' and the reader is left to gather the meaning from the context, or to look in the dictionary. A *desultory conversation* is one which shifts erratically from one subject to another: Bulwer-Lytton provides a contextual hint to make it clear in *The Last Days of Pompeii*: 'The conversation, at first desultory and scattered …'

How many people can, with confidence, distinguish between *venal* and *venial*? Both seem bad, but which is worse and why? *Venal* comes from the Latin *venum*, 'that which is exposed for sale': a cousin to *vendor* and *vending* machine. Although the nation of shopkeepers has nothing against commerce as such, *venal* gradually drifted south: things exposed for sale; offices or privileges available for purchase; a person open to bribery; and finally its current, unsavoury meaning, 'Connected or associated with sordid and unprincipled bargaining; subject to mercenary or corrupt influences'.

Tacitus wrote in the *Annals*: 'of all articles of public merchandise nothing was more venal than the treachery of advocates.'

By contrast, *venial* comes from *venia*: indulgence or forgiveness. So, of any offence, sin, lapse, or error it signifies the non-conviction-bond end of the scale. Chaucer commented that 'sin is of two kinds; it is either venial or mortal sin.' This is the problem with *venial*: it is very often associated with sin, and takes an unhealthy taint from it. Boswell avoided confusion when he referred to Johnson as imagining '*such little venial trifles* as pouring milk into his tea on Good-Friday'.

Tacitus was needlessly harsh on advocates. Johnson was not keen on them, either. He once observed that '… he did not care to speak ill of any man behind his back, but he believed the gentleman was an attorney.' Possibly Boswell, who was an advocate, helped adjust Johnson's attitude. Johnson understood better than Tacitus that there is no difficulty in taking an unworthy or unpopular cause:

A lawyer has no business with the justice or injustice of the cause which he undertakes, unless his client asks his opinion, and then he is bound to give it honestly. The justice or injustice of the cause is to be decided by the judge.

(James Boswell, *Journal of a Tour to the Hebrides with Samuel Johnson, LL.D*, 1785)

ODDS AND ENDS

———◆———

The internet has become very popular recently. Everyone has heard about it, and many use it daily. With it has come email, with its address template addressee@server.com. The form is universal, so much so that most word-processors automatically give an expression in that form an email hyperlink. Nevertheless, the @ which unequivocally marks it as an email address has no generally accepted English name.

Officially, it is called the *atmark*, or *commercial at*. If you think these names are widely known, just try using one of them when giving an email address, and see the confusion it causes.

Other languages are not so restrained. In Italian, it is called *chiocciola* (little snail); in Dutch it is an *aperstaart* (monkey's tail); and in Swedish, it is a *snabel-a* ('a' with an elephant's trunk), or *kanelbulle* (the Swedish equivalent of the Chelsea bun). Using the same metaphor, it is a *strudel* in Yiddish; in German it is *eine Klammeraffe* (a clinging monkey); in Finnish, it is a *monkey's tail;* in Greek it is a *duck;* and in Russian it is a *dog.*

One observer has suggested that it should be an *ampersat* in English, which avoids the frivolity of the Europeans, and claims legitimacy by familiarity. It does not have a common heritage with the *ampersand (&)*, but no matter.

The *ampersand* used to be part of the alphabet learned at school by children. When reciting the alphabet, they would recite A *per se* A, B *per se* B … meaning, '*A* as a word by itself is pronounced *A* …', etc. The last term in the series was *& per se and.* Before long, repeated incantation had worn it down to *ampersand.*

❧

There are other common things that we all recognise but cannot name. For example, an obvious feature of every person's face is the vertical groove from the nose to the upper lip. It is part of the natural topology of shaving, or applying lipstick. It is the *philtrum,* and you will find reference to it in Nathaniel Bailey's *English Dictionary* (1742). Nevertheless, it does not appear in Johnson (1755), nor in the *OED2,* nor Webster. However, for recent verification, you will find it in the second edition of the *Random House Dictionary of the English Language.*

The word *lace* has several quite different meanings. The original sense is *a cord or thread*, especially for drawing edges together by passing it through eyelets. It comes from the Latin *laqueum (lacium)*: a noose. From the thirteenth century the word meant a cord or thread, but also meant a *net, snare,* or *noose. Lasso* gets its meaning directly from this (see 'Self-Contradicting Words').

St Aetheldreda (St Audrey) wore a silken cord around her neck, and when she developed a tumour of the throat she attributed it to this vanity. The style came to be called *St Audrey's lace*, and later *tawdry lace*. Apparently the quality of tawdry lace sold at the markets fell in quality to the point where *tawdry* no longer has any sense of quality or fineness.

By skilful use of a thread and needle, an open-work fabric can be made, and by transfer of ideas this came to be called *lace*.

Corsets, stays, and other garments used to be fastened with laces. If fastened tightly, they would necessarily have constricted movement. It is not difficult to imagine the personal psychology of a person who chose to have their stays laced excessively tightly. Since *strait* means narrow or tight (as in the *Straits of Gibraltar*, and *in straitened circumstances*) a person disposed to over-tighten their stay-laces was described as *strait-laced*.

Another meaning of *lace* (used as a verb) is *to beat* or *thrash*, and in eighteenth-century cooking circles it meant *to make a number of incisions in the breast of a bird*. It is possible that these meanings arise from a confusion with *lash,* since the sounds are similar, and in nautical use *lashing* (whether beating a person or making fast a piece of equipment) involves the use of a cord. The temptation to assume that *lacerate* is a related word is understandable, but wrong.

But how to explain *lace* in the usage *lace a person's drink*? In *The Private Lives of English Words* (Heller & Ors, 1984), the authors suggest that it comes from the fact that the drink is embellished by the illicit additive. Possible, but not really convincing. An alternative explanation might be that, for a time, *lace* was also used to mean *sugar*. In 1687, Miege's *French Dictionary* translated 'to lace coffee' as *mettre un peu de sucre dans une tasse de caphe*. Johnson also treats *lace* as meaning *sugar* in the same context, but says the usage is obsolete. *Lace* got this meaning from a closely related Latin origin: *lacere* (to snare), whence *delicere* (to divert by trickery). From this we get *delicious*, *delicacy*, and (via German) *delicatessen*.

And what about those handy little things at the end of shoelaces which make it easier to thread them through the eyelets? They are *aglets,* and are recognised in Bailey, Johnson, Webster, and the *OED2*.

And now for something completely different.

I am not normally much interested in word-games of the form, 'What are the only three words in the English language which end with the letters *-gry*?' Still, most rules have exceptions, and for no obvious reason I was interested to read recently a discussion of the appearance of concatenations of consonants in English words.

It is notorious that some eastern European languages manage to string together impossibly large collections of consonants unrelieved by vowels. We generally assume that English confines itself to two or three consonants at a time. So, *consonants* ends with a string of three consonants, a pattern which is not obvious, but not uncommon. A little thought on the problem leads us to *rhythm*, which might be said to have six consonants in a row. However, there is a trick in this word, arising from the fact that the letter Y in English does double service, both as a consonant and as a quasi-vowel. No other English letter has this dual characteristic, although *i* and *j* were treated as facets of the same letter until the early nineteenth century. For a purist, then, *tachydysrhythmia* (rapid heart beats resulting from psychological disturbance) is stripped of its otherwise distinguished position of having nine consonants in a row. However, even excluding words that depend on the vocalic *y*, it is possible to find English words which contain six consonants in a row. There are two such words at least which are in very common use: *catchphrase* and *watchstrap*.

ROMANTIC ORIGINS

————◆————

The origins of many words are fascinating, even romantic. As various words become familiar in daily use, their histories are all but forgotten. I will admit to a personal favourite: *halcyon*. *Halcyon* suffers a double injury — not only is its romantic history generally unknown; its true meaning is often mistaken.

Halcyon is now seen only in the idiom *the halcyon days*, although it was once used as a noun. It is generally used as referring to days distant and more pleasant, shrouded in the contentment of selective memory. Properly used, it refers to the 14 days of calm weather at sea which, according to Greek legend, interrupt the storms of mid-winter. It comes from *hals*: salt, or the sea and *kuo*: to brood on. According to Greek legend, the kingfisher makes its nest on the water and hatches its eggs during the 14 days of calm at mid-winter. Properly used, *halcyon* means the tranquil spell surrounding the winter solstice.

Halcyon was the daughter of Neptune, keeper of the seas. She fell in love with Ceyx, the mortal king of Thessaly. Ceyx went to sea and was shipwrecked. His body was washed ashore, where Halcyon found it. Distracted by grief, she took his corpse into the water, wishing for death to reunite them. But the gods took pity on her and turned the two of them into kingfishers. Out on the stormy seas, the two kingfishers mated, and made a nest on the sea. Neptune, concerned for his grandchildren, stilled the waves while the eggs hatched. The sea was still for 14 days — the halcyon days. The zoological name for the kingfisher, incidentally, is *Halcyon*.

Thus, Dryden wrote (of Cromwell):

And wars have that respect for his repose
As winds for halcyons when they breed at sea

and Shenstone:

So smiles the surface of the treach'rous main,
As o'er its waves the peaceful halcyons play.

Another, much commoner, word with classical origins is *clue*. Until very recently, it was spelt *clew*: the 1902 edition of Webster's dictionary gives *clew* as the primary spelling; the 1933 *Shorter OED* likewise.

The current primary meaning is something which guides or directs in anything of a doubtful or intricate nature, or which gives a hint of the solution to a mystery.

But until recently that was the secondary meaning. The primary meaning from the twelfth century to the end of the nineteenth century was a ball of thread or twine. In Scotland and the north of England, *clew* still bears that meaning.

The connection between the two meanings comes from ancient Greece by way of Chaucer. Theseus, after a difficult childhood, set himself a number of heroic tasks. The greatest was to slay the Cretan Minotaur. The Minotaur lived in a labyrinth, which presented difficulties for anyone wishing to do the deed and see daylight again. Minos, the King of Crete, demanded that Theseus be sacrificed to the Minotaur. However, Minos' daughter Ariadne fell in love with Theseus, and gave him two things to ensure his survival: a sword to slay the monster, and a ball of thread. He paid out the thread as he walked into the labyrinth, and used it to retrace his steps after slaying the Minotaur. He then took Ariadne away with him, but left her at Naxos, where she took up with the fun-loving Dionysus.

In *Legends of a Good Woman*, Chaucer wrote:

… by a clewe of twine as he hath gon
The same way he may return anon
Followinge alway the thread as he hath come.

Thus the figurative sense was introduced. To all but the most pedantic, the figurative sense has overwhelmed the original literal sense. Nevertheless, the *OED2* (1989) gives as the first definition of *clue*: 'A ball of yarn or thread'.

SELF-CONTRADICTING WORDS

—————◆—————

In the preface to his great *Dictionary of the English Language*, Dr Johnson wrote:

> I am not yet so lost in lexicography, as to forget that words are the daughters of earth, and that things are the sons of heaven. Language is only the instrument of science, and words are but the signs of ideas: I wish, however, that the instrument might be less apt to decay, and that signs might be permanent, like the things which they denote.

Change in language provoked despair in Johnson, irritation in Fowler, and impotent rage in those many who would see the language fixed as it was when they finished their formal education.

Rapid and mindless change in usage and vocabulary certainly causes inconvenience: it disguises or distorts meaning where the true object of language is to convey meaning as clearly as human frailty allows. On the other hand, gradual evolution of language — even by the adoption of 'barbarisms' — helps ensure its continued vigour. The English language is a perfect example.

Change in language also gives scope for minor fossicking and diversions for those who amuse themselves with such things. It is a commonplace that the meaning of a word may change over time. In some words, the change may be very dramatic. In a few cases, the meaning may reverse itself entirely.

Thus, *obnoxious* originally means 'exposed to harm, subject to a harmful or evil influence or agency' (*OED2*, 1989; and it was so used in the *Law Times* as late as 1891).

The *Macquarie Dictionary* (second edition, 1991) gives the primary meaning as 'objectionable, offensive, odious'; and the secondary meaning as 'exposed or liable' (to harm, evil, or anything objectionable).

Another well-known example is *prestige*: originally 'juggling or magic; cheating, deluding, deceitful' (*OED2*, 1989). Now: 'reputation or influence arising from success, influence, rank or other circumstances' (Macquarie 1991).

Other examples are *panache* and *mere*.

A more controversial example is *tawdry* (see p 171). It is a contraction of St Audrey (St Aethelthreda) who, according to the Venerable Bede, died in 679 as a result of a growth on her throat. This she attributed to her early vanity of wearing a silken lace around her neck. The monastery she established at Ely became the famous cathedral, where a fair was held each 17 October in honour of her memory. Gold jewellery was sold as *St Audrey's lace* and then *taudry lace* in memory of the supposed cause of her death. It was not necessarily cheap and showy, but it quickly gained that reputation. Despite an ambiguous quotation from Wycherley in 1676 ('taudry affected rogues, well drest') the *OED2* admits only a pejorative meaning of the word; but it admits equally that *taudry lace* — the original expression — once denoted real finery.

A word with several meanings is said to be *polysemous* (an expression adopted by practitioners of modern linguistics; not recognised by the first edition of the *OED*, but first recorded in 1884, according to the second edition). The words discussed above, however, take their polysemic character to a hermaphroditic extreme. Commentators (Philip Howard, Tom McArthur, and others) have tried to popularise *Janus word* as a description of this little linguistic curiosity. On the Humpty Dumpty principle, any word would do, provided we decide what it should mean. On the other hand, *enantiodromic* has a long and honourable history, and seems to do the work for which *Janus word* was coined.

The enantiodromic word is only one species of polysemy. The creature has relatives who bear a striking but spurious resemblance. For example, *to cleave* means 'to part or divide by a cutting blow, to hew asunder, to split; but also to stick fast or adhere'.

Although apparently the same word with opposite meanings, they are etymologically distinct, having converged on a common form from separate origins. The first sense derives from the old English *cliofan*; the second, from old

English *clifan*. This branch of the family is the *homonym*.

Other, but less challenging, members of the family are *homophones* and *homographs*. They comprise pairs (or groups) of words that are entirely separate in meaning and etymology, but happen to look and/or sound identical.

Hence:

sow (spread seed) / *sow* (female pig);
lead (conduct) / *lead* (metal);
bear (carry) / *bear* (animal);
swallow (ingest) / *swallow* (bird), and so on.

Perhaps the most interesting form of polysemous word is the subspecies in which the one word bears two current meanings which are diametrically opposed. Enantiodromic words show historical drift; this subspecies, however, maintains the two opposite meanings side by side. These are, of necessity, rare creatures, and yet some of them pass unnoticed every day. Thus:

fast: firmly fixed in its place; not easily
                 moved or shaken
              settled, stable
              quick, swift, moving quickly

quite: completely, wholly, altogether, entirely
              to the fullest extent or degree
              rather, to a moderate degree, fairly

to sanction: to ratify or confirm; to make valid or
                binding
                to enforce a law by attaching a penalty to
                transgression

to weather: to subject to the beneficial action of the
                wind and the sun
                to change by exposure to the weather, to
                wear away, disintegrate
                to withstand and come safely through (a
                storm)
                to sustain without disaster

This branch of the family has also been labelled *Janus words*. Possibly a more accurate, and already available, expression is *amphibolous words*.

Polysemous words lace our language, yet ideas can be unequivocally expressed. Context almost invariably provides the clue to enable the intended meaning of a polysemic word to be determined. It is a fascinating exercise — and a very difficult one — to construct a sentence of ten words or more which is truly ambiguous.

SHE/HE/THEY

———————◆———————

'If a person makes a contract for provision of services, he she or it must register that contract with the office of …'

'If a person makes a contract for provision of services, they must register that contract with the office of …'

Which of the above is to be preferred? The latest and most troublesome shibboleth in the English language is the use of the indeterminate third-person singular pronoun: a singular third-person pronoun equally applicable to masculine, feminine, or neuter subjects. Since feminist writers drew our attention to the fact that the English language has deeply ingrained male-biased conventions, those of us with a conscience have tried to find a way of compensating for our lack of a pronoun that applies equally to male or female referents. For centuries, legal statutes were an obvious example of the problem:

If a person does such-and-such, he is guilty of an offence.

To avoid the obvious difficulties, a reference to the male was defined as including the female. A new drafting style, which has recently been adopted in most jurisdictions, is to say *he or she; him or her; his or hers,* wherever there is a reference to the third-person singular. Presumably, companies are thereby attributed masculine or feminine gender.

This is increasingly used in other fields of discourse; even (occasionally) barristers speaking in court will use this new, inclusive expression. Cutting-edge practitioners of modern English are consciously using *she or he* in the same circumstances, on the footing that *he or she* still contains the residue of male bias.

This is all very commendable, and it has achieved some small measure of success, but it is ugly and cumbersome. It is the only pronoun with more than one syllable, and only an enthusiast could use the new construction without a sidelong glance at its aesthetic effect.

Consider, for example, Keats' *The Human Seasons* (my alterations are in italics):

Four seasons fill the measure of the year;
There are four seasons in the mind of *man or woman*:
He or she has *his or her* lusty Spring, when fancy clear
Takes in all beauty with an easy span:
He or she has *his or her* Summer, when luxuriously
Spring's honey'd cud of youthful thought *he or she* loves
To ruminate, and by such dreaming high
Is nearest unto heaven: quiet coves

His or her soul has in its Autumn, when *his or her* wings
He or she furleth close; contented so to look
On mists in idleness- to let fair things
Pass by unheeded as a threshold brook.
He or she has *his or her* Winter too of pale misfeature,
Or else *he or she* would forego *his or her* mortal nature.

Many other solutions to the problem have been advanced from time to time. *S/he*, which was urged in the early days of the new consciousness, was visually effective, but unpronounceable. Other offerings include *tey*, *co*, *per*, and *E*. None of these has so far caught on.

The alternative to these worthy but unsuccessful constructions is to use the gender-neutral plurals: *they*, *them*, *their*. These indeterminate pronouns are a useful, and aesthetically acceptable solution to a real problem. The purists complain that the plural pronoun cannot — simply cannot — be used with reference to a singular noun. This complaint, however, founders on three points:

- English displays idiosyncrasies in many matters, so disagreement of number is not, of itself, impermissibly odd;
- plurals, in English, are fraught with exceptions and anomalies in any event; and
- the language needs a gender-neutral third-person singular pronoun, and pressing the plural into service on aesthetic grounds has a long and distinguished history.

The first proposition needs no proof. The second is dealt with briefly in 'Strange Plurals'. The third is more interesting, because the purists castigate the indeterminate pronoun as a grammatically unacceptable modernism. In fact, it has been used for centuries by the best writers in the English language. In each of the following examples, grammatical convention requires a singular pronoun:

1464: *Rolls of Parliament*: 'Inheritements, of which any of the seid persones ... was seised by **theym self**, or joyntly with other.' (V. 513/2)

1470: *Caxton*: 'Each of **them** should make **themself** ready';

1594: *Shakespeare*: 'There's not a man I meet but doth salute me, As if I were **their** well-acquainted friend.' (*Comedy of Errors*, Act IV Scene 3)

1598: *Shakespeare*: 'God send every one **their** heart's desire.' (*Much Ado About Nothing*, Act 3 sc. iv)

1611: *The Bible (authorised version)*: 'Let nothing be done through strife or vainglory; but in lowliness of mind let each esteem other better than **them**selves.' (*Philippians* 2:3)

1749: *Fielding*, 'Every Body fell a laughing, as how could **they** help it.' (*Tom Jones* viii. xi)

1759 *Chesterfield*: 'If a person is born of a ... gloomy temper ... **they** cannot help it.' (*Letters* IV. ccclv. 170)

1813: *Jane Austen*: 'I always delight in overthrowing those kind of schemes, and cheating a person of **their** premeditated contempt.' (*Pride and Prejudice*)

1817: *Jane Austen*: 'She did not blame Lady Russell, she did not blame herself for having been guided by her; but she felt that were any young person, in similar circumstances, to apply to her for counsel, they would never receive any of such certain immediate wretchedness, such uncertain future good.' (*Persuasion*)

1858: *Bagehot*: 'Nobody fancies for a moment that **they** are reading about anything beyond the pale of ordinary propriety.' (*Literary Studies* II. 206)

1866: *Ruskin*: 'Now, nobody does anything well that **they** cannot help doing.' (*Crown of Wild Olives* §38)

Parallel examples for *them* and *their* abound from the fifteenth to the nineteenth centuries.

Recently, the example of great writers has offered an elegant solution to the problem identified by the feminists. But the purists reacted with vehement opposition. Why?

It is, I believe, a legacy of the great push to regularise English. In the eighteenth century, grammar was the new growth industry; indeed, a quick look at a good dictionary reveals that most technical expressions in grammar date from that century. Grammarians had appointed themselves to establish a system of rules for the English language. This they did by analogy with Latin, regardless of the differences between the two languages. They decreed, for example, that an English infinitive could not be split, because a Latin infinitive could not be split (see pp 159–160). This mindless decree overlooks the fact that in Latin, unlike English, the infinitive is a single word, so of course it could not be split.

They decreed that a preposition could not be placed at the end of a sentence, because Latin construction did not permit terminal prepositions. This completely ignores the existence, in the mongrel English, of phrasal verbs, such as *put up with*, *run away*, *sleep over*, etc., where the function of the prepositions has no direct equivalent in Latin. Churchill famously parodied this pedantic dictate, saying that 'This is the sort of English up with which I will not put.'

In the same way, the grammarians insisted that the pronoun should be singular if it corresponded to a singular noun. As a principle, this cannot be criticised. However, grammatical irregularity alone need not result in automatic banishment. If it were otherwise, a large part of the language would disappear. The case for many irregularities in English is no more than an acknowledgement of historical fact: that is how it is.

In the matter of plurals, English excels itself in its wilful disregard of rules. But the case for the indeterminate pronoun is strong: it has a long history; it avoids the need to specify sex where to do so may be impossible, meaningless, or offensive; and it does this without damaging the aesthetic balance of the sentence. If a purist cannot embrace this usage, they should at least tolerate it.

If anyone wants to use the indeterminate pronoun, I will support them.

Incidentally, I have been cautious in this essay about the word *gender*. *Gender* is a word that is undergoing significant change as part of the feminist awareness of bias in language. *Gender* and *sex* are not synonyms. They should not be used interchangeably.

Sex is a characteristic of organisms. It distinguishes between *male* and *female*.

Gender is a grammatical construct: it distinguishes between the two (or, in many languages, three) grammatical 'kinds', *masculine*, *feminine*, and *neuter*. Although these kinds generally agree with the corresponding distinctions of sex, this is not always so. In many languages that retain distinctions of gender there are anomalous cases where sex and gender do not correspond. In German, the word for young girls is neuter (*das Mädchen*). In English, animals (and babies) are often referred to as *it* (neuter), even though their sex may be known; and ships and cars are generally treated as feminine, although they plainly have no sex.

The modern use of *gender* as meaning *sex* can be dated to the early 1960s and the beginnings of modern feminism. It was originally a euphemism for *sex*. Like most euphemisms, it serves to protect the susceptible. But euphemisms blunt meaning, and weaken useful distinctions.

Sex and *gender* are not the same. It is better to distinguish them than to confuse them.

SHIFTING SANDS

———◆———

It is a wonder that we manage to communicate more or less successfully, so many are the changes in the meaning of words over time. The shift of meaning causes special problems for lawyers as they struggle to draw sensible or convenient meanings from statutes or contracts. The difficulty increases in proportion to the age of the document to be construed.

Luckily for our daily conversation, the shift of meaning usually takes decades or centuries, although newly minted words often go through an early period of instability.

Documents written before the start of the nineteenth century are likely to present familiar words whose context will make the astute reader pause to wonder what the writer truly meant. For example, in *Henry VI* Part 1, Shakespeare has York address Joan of Arc ('la Pucelle') as *miscreant*. While he may have disagreed with her views or her conduct, *miscreant* in its modern sense (*OED2*: depraved, villainous, base) seems not to be what York intended.

Similarly, but less clearly, Lear's exchange with Kent:

Kent: Now by Apollo, King,
     Thou swearst thy gods in vain.
Lear: O vassal! Miscreant!

The original sense is 'false believer'. In times when religious belief was more important than it is now, it was natural that the word acquired the strong pejorative sense given it by Johnson: 'a vile wretch'. The original meaning dates from the early fourteenth century and was current until the mid-nineteenth century. The current meaning emerged at the end of the sixteenth century. Thus, both senses were current when Shakespeare wrote. It seems clear that he intended York's comment in the original sense. Lear's comment is made in response to a comment about religious belief, but it may be that he was so vexed by daughters and circumstances that he intended the modern meaning and a blunt insult.

I have discussed elsewhere the slow decline of *tawdry*. *St Audrey-Lace* was fine and pure, but eventually cheapened to *tawdry lace*. *Tinsel* has followed the same path. Now meaning cheap and showy (unfairly attached to Sydney, which Melburnians refer to as Tinsel Town) it once had something of the divine spark. It comes into English from old French *estincelle* that in turn traces back to Latin *scintillare*: to sparkle or glitter. From the same root we have *scintilla*: a spark ('not a scintilla of evidence'), and *scintillating* ('brilliantly and excitingly clever, especially in conversation').

This last definition, which is the current popular sense of *scintillating* comes from the *New Oxford Dictionary of English* (1998). It has no equivalent in the *OED2* (1989). A similar sense is recognised by the *Chambers Dictionary* (1993), the *American Heritage Dictionary* (2000), and the *Macquarie Dictionary* (second edition, 1991; third edition, 1997). The *Random House Dictionary* (second edition, 1987) also recognises this sense, as does the *Webster's Encyclopaedic Dictionary* of the same year.

It would be misleading to say this gap in the *OED2* is baffling — at least, it would have been until the mid-seventeenth century. Originally, *baffle* had nothing to do with confusion or puzzlement. It referred to the treatment of a knight who had dishonoured his chivalrous obligations: he was (in person or in effigy) hung up by the heels, his escutcheon was defaced and his spear broken; he (or his effigy) was then subjected to the abuse and humiliations of the crowd. The person subjected to these indignities was said to have been *baffled*, and a *baffle* was a disgrace or an affront. By the time of *Bailey's Dictionary* (tenth edition, 1742) and Johnson (1755) the only sense recognised was the modern one. Presumably this was for either of two reasons: the age of chivalry had passed, and its usages had lost their relevance; or knights of the realm had so improved their behaviour as to make their public disgrace no longer relevant.

Perhaps the knights exercised their influence at court to change the system. In those days however, *influence* had a somewhat different meaning: it was the ethereal liquid which was thought to flow from the stars and so affect the character and destiny of men and the behaviour of 'sub-lunary things' generally. In short, *influence* was the force that underpins the pseudo-science of astrology. Strictly, mortals could not exercise influence, but were subject to it. Modern times have reversed that — we seek to influence others and deny the theories of the astrologers.

Early medicine thought that disease could be caused by these forces from the stars. The Italian for *influence* is *influenza*. When an epidemic of one disease or another swept the country, it was referred to as an *influenza di febbre scarlatina*, or an *influenza di catarro*, and so on.

In 1743, an epidemic spread across Italy and then the rest of Europe. A report in the *London Magazine* referred to 'News from Rome of a contagious Distemper raging there, called the *Influenza*'. The name stuck, and became specific to the particular viral infection whose symptoms are now well known. Later epidemics occurred in 1762, 1782, 1787, 1803, 1833, 1837, 1847, and a particularly bad one in 1889. The worst recorded epidemic of influenza was in 1918, in which 30 million people died.

Note that in the *London Magazine* the catarrh-like disease was referred to as a *Distemper* — a word which then signified any 'deranged or disordered condition of the body or mind'. Its primary sense now is the specific catarrh-like disease of dogs (and, according to the *Macquarie Dictionary*, horses).

Originally, a distemper was thought to result from a disordered state of the humours. The *humours* were the four fluids of the body: blood, phlegm, choler, and black choler. *Choler* is bile. *Melos* is Greek for *black*, so black bile is *melancholy.* Thus the human tempers associated with the four humours were *sanguine, phlegmatic, choleric* (or *bilious*), and *melancholy.*

Each of these words is familiar, but they are not now used as diagnostic tools. Only *sanguine* presents linguistic problems: because of its connexion with blood, it has oddly ambiguous meanings. As a humour, people in whom it predominates are thought to have 'a ruddy complexion and a courageous, hopeful, and amorous disposition'. However, it also means 'causing or delighting in bloodshed, bloody-minded'. Thus, unless the context resolves the ambiguity, describing a person as *sanguine* may not improve their humour.

Although the primary current sense of *humour* concerns mirth or amusement (its adjective *humorous* has only that sense), the earlier sense is called on when we speak of ill-humour or bad humour.

And so the process goes — words shed old meanings and take on new ones, and it happens slowly enough that we can keep pace with the fashion (*fashion*: originally the action or process of making something, a sense retained in the verb *to fashion* a thing). Our language is built on shifting sands.

Paradoxically, the current sense of the word *sand* has been stable since the ninth century.

SLANG #1

All living languages change, but the rate of change is variable between languages and within particular languages. Italian, for example, changed much less between the fourteenth and twentieth centuries than English did during the same period. As a result, fourteenth-century Italian is readily understood by an intelligent Italian speaker, but Chaucer is virtually impenetrable to most English speakers.

Different registers of language show different degrees of volatility. Informal registers (especially slang) are much more volatile than more formal registers such as the language of law.

It is at the boundary between formal and informal registers that change causes most confusion and irritation. Use of colloquialisms in court or in polite society is a dangerous activity. Even so, some colloquialisms pass into accepted use, while others remain outside the bounds of formal registers. *Fax* has made the transition; *mobile* (as a noun, for mobile phone) has not made the transition, but is likely to. (Note that *phone* has so completely moved into proper use that *'phone* or *telephone* seem affected or overly formal).

Slang is an interesting object of study precisely because it is so volatile. It offers a speeded-up view of the processes of language change. Perhaps not surprisingly, some slang expressions gain wide currency for a time, and then disappear. When encountered afterwards, they date the speaker or writer as effectively as flared jeans. *Flapper, 23 skidoo, zounds, dinky-di*, and *zoot suit* all carry with them a sense of another time and place.

Australian English was once very rich in slang. It is less so now. In part, this is a result of inventiveness being overtaken by laziness. *Shit* and *fuck*, alone or in compound expressions, now dominate slang speech. Each is now used as virtually every part of speech other than particle and preposition. This is unfortunate: they are losing their edge.

In part, the growing poverty of Australian slang may be due to television, which represents an increasing component of the verbal input of most people. Television undoubtedly uses a narrow and safe vocabulary. Baker (*The Australian Language*, 1945) complained that 'the American talkie is exerting the worst possible influence on Australian speech'. The same is true of television, but more so.

The world's most durable slang expression is *OK*. It was coined in 1839, and is now universally used and understood.

Australia has coined some pretty durable slang expressions such as *mate, furphy, come in spinner,* and *Buckley's chance.* However, whether a slang expression survives or fades is a chancy business. Consider the following:

afto (1945): afternoon (now *arvo*)

(Prince) Alberts (1945): foot rags worn by swagmen or tramps

tinarse/tinny (1918): unusually lucky (now *arsey*)

boko (?1945): blind in one eye

borak (1845): taunting words

have the bot (1941): to be ill, especially gastric disorder

tie up a dog (1937) drink at a pub on credit (hence *the dogs are barking* meant the publican wanted payment forthwith)

bumper (1916): cigarette end

gooly/brinnie (1941): a stone or pebble (now, or until recently, *yonnie*)

trey (1859): threepenny piece

zac (1898): sixpenny piece

deener (1839): one shilling

frog/quid: one pound note

These were once in common use. The *OED2* (1989) identifies 852 words or expressions (from *abo* to *ziff*) as Australian slang — many of them no longer current. Baker, in 1945, asserted that there were about 7000 Australian slang and colloquial expressions. In *The Drum* (1959) he lists 1258 slang expressions. (How many people under 40 now recognise, let alone use, the slang expression *drum*?)

In 1942, Jim Donald wrote in *Truth* an example of then current slang:

> I'm dropping briefs at the fight and someone drums me there's two Jacks on my hammer. I palm the briefs and front 'em and I'm a quick jerry they ain't coppers. When I tail 'em and sight 'em buyin' their ducats for the brawl, I know I'm sweet — Jacks never pay for anything.

This was nothing if not dated. By contrast, consider the following:

black stump (1826)
bush (1826)
billy (1839)
yacker (1888); *yakker* (1948); *yakka* (1968)
nick off (1896)
bludge (1919)
bot (1919) (in the sense of borrowing)
woop woop (1926)
pissed (1929)
put your bib in (1959)
big note (1959)

I'll make a billy of tea, OK? uses two slang words, both first recorded in 1839. It would *pass muster* (1627) without comment. If you say *maleesh* (1919) to a *reffo* (1945), he may understand, but your Australian audience probably won't.

It was Michael Pearce, a barrister at the Victorian Bar,who prompted me to write something about slang. He sent me a cutting from the *New York Times* (24 June 1994) which used the recent Australianism *sledging*. Pearce pointed out that the expression has gained currency in sporting circles in the UK and USA. It is not recognised in *OED2* (1989). Certainly it has spread beyond sports in Australian usage. It has the merit of being concise, self-explanatory, and applicable to a favourite Australian practice. It will probably survive.

Those are the three essential conditions for the survival of a slang expression. Social change is probably the main influence in the life-cycle of slang words. For example, the move from the bush to the city has stripped away the context and purpose of hundreds of once-common expressions, while the conditions of war produced many expressions that survived only in the memory of diggers once taken to a civilian setting:

> *Anzac button*: a nail used in place of a button;
> *branding paddock*: parade ground;
> *camel dung*: Egyptian cigarette;
> *cream puff*: shell burst;
> *pongo*: soldier (rank and file);
> *rissole king*: army cook;
> *shining stars*: commissioned officer;
> *souvy*: to steal;
> *throw a seven*: die;

throw six and a half: almost die; and

treacle miner: a person who brags about his position in civilian life.

The depressions of the 1890s and 1930s produced slang that ceased to have much relevance when prosperity returned. It has not revived during the depression of the 1990s, perhaps because the *dole* (1205) had replaced *susso* (1930s); the *Salvos* (1896) distribute shoes to those who would otherwise have been *toe-raggers* (1896); the *rabbit-o* (1908) now has a stall at the Victoria Market.

Two major exceptions are *swagman* and *matilda* (swag) which emerged in the 1890s, but were immortalised by Banjo Paterson in 1917. Equivalent expressions from the same time, but now forgotten, include *bender, drummer, scowbanker, scullbanker, sundodger,* and *coiler* (for *swagman*); and *bundle, curse, shiralee, turkey,* and *donkey* (for *swag*).

❧

I mentioned the *furphy* earlier. Its origins are widely known. John Furphy of Shepparton made the cast-iron water carts that carried water to the troops at Gallipoli. One of the carts can still be seen in Shepparton, and the foundry still operates there.

Because the water cart was a natural gathering point, and because it moved regularly from place to place, it became the agency by which news was spread. Since the news was often unreliable, the name *furphy* was attached to any false rumour. (A parallel construction is found in *scuttlebutt* — originally, the scuttle-butt was a cask of water on board a ship, where sailors drew their drinking water.) What is less well known is an odd linguistic coincidence behind *furphy*. There had been several earlier slang expressions for false rumours or exaggerated stories, among them *mulga wire, bush wire,* and *Tom Collins.* The last was derived from the pen-name of the author of *Such is Life* (1903) whose eponymous hero's exploits stretched credulity. Tom Collins also wrote far-fetched stories for the *Bulletin* during the 1890s. Tom Collins was a pseudonym for Joseph Furphy — brother of John, at whose foundry he worked for some years during the 1880s. So the Furphy brothers between them managed to give our language two slang expressions for the same idea.

SLANG #2

———◆———

What constitutes slang is difficult to identify precisely. The word *slang* is not recognised by Johnson (1755) — except as the preterite of the verb *sling* (*sling-slang-slung*, on the same pattern as *ring-rang-rung*): 'David slang a stone and smote the Philistine'. Nathaniel Bailey (1742) does not mention the word at all. The earliest quotation supplied by the *OED2* dates to 1756, and it does not offer an etymology for the word.

The *OED2* rather loftily defines *slang* as 'the special vocabulary used by any set of persons of a low or disreputable character; language of a low or vulgar type'. It gives a later meaning as 'the special vocabulary or phraseology of a particular calling or profession'. That later definition has *slang* indistinguishable from *jargon*.

Eric Partridge, in his *Dictionary of Slang and Unconventional English*, gives a fair working idea of slang's boundaries. He distinguishes as follows: slang and cant, colloquialisms, solecisms and catachreses, catchphrases, nicknames, and vulgarisms. This nice subdivision is probably the best guide to the nature of slang.

Carl Sandburg captured the spirit of slang when he said 'slang is a language that rolls up its sleeves, spits on its hands and goes to work'. By contrast, G.K. Chesterton wrote 'All slang is metaphor, and all metaphor is poetry'. Not many would equate slang with poetry, even obliquely.

However defined, slang is an informal register — one which makes its own rules, but steers clear of open vulgarity. Because it is homemade, jury-rigged language, it tends to be blunt, honest, and unfinished.

Slang develops as capriciously as language in more formal registers, but the whole process is accelerated. Slang words emerge when circumstances are right; they change form or meaning quickly as their use spreads; and they flourish or they disappear — sometimes within a generation or two. Time and circumstances dictate which slang words are coined; chance and fashion dictate which words survive.

The following slang words all emerged at about the same time (1900–1920, but especially during the First World War). Some are so familiar as to have passed into more formal registers; others are completely forgotten, except among war veterans or their families:

> *welter* ('to make a welter of it': to go to extremes, take
>   excessive trouble);
> *bonzer*: extremely good;
> *boshter, bosker*: bonzer;

dinkum (adjective): genuine;
dinkum (noun): work, especially hard work;
beetle about: to move about rapidly;
blotto, blithered, inked, oiled, molo, perked: drunk;
kip (noun): sleep; also, a brothel;
kip (verb): to lodge or sleep; to play truant;
kipsey: a house or home; and
offsider: assistant

It is surprising to learn that *welter* and *offsider* were originally — and recently — slang words. Likewise, it is curious that the noun form of *dinkum* has virtually disappeared, and that the only meaning of *kip* which currently survives is *sleep* in a neutral sense.

Bouncer is no longer regarded as slang: the *Macquarie Dictionary* (third edition, 1997) defines it without comment, as does the *New Oxford Dictionary of English* (1998). But it was treated as slang as recently as 1989 (second edition *Oxford English Dictionary*), and likewise was recorded as slang by Eric Partridge (1951) and by Downing in *Digger Dialects* (1919). It has an entry in Francis Grose's *Dictionary of the Vulgar Tongue* (1811).

This recent respectability of *bouncer* is a strange thing, because its current meaning is both colloquial and recent. From the early nineteenth century, *bouncer* had two meanings:

- a large, swaggering or boastful person
- a great lie or deception

In those senses it was treated as slang until recent times. The original meaning of *bouncer* is noted in Johnson (1755) and in the 1902 edition of Webster.

Bouncer is now fairly specific: a person employed by a nightclub or similar establishment to exclude patrons who may drink too little, and to expel those who have drunk too much. The original bouncer was a swaggering bully. Social Darwinism ensured that such people were physically strong (others had the tendency knocked out of them). The physical characteristics of swaggering bullies were thought useful at nightclubs, and the meaning shifted to suit the new reality. The current sense emerged in Australia and the US at about the time of the First World War. The English slang equivalent is *chucker out*.

Other bits of World War I slang that have survived and flourished include:

cobber: friend;
furphy: false or exaggerated story (see pp 199–200);
banger: sausage;
buzz off: go away;
nut it out: think a problem through to its conclusion; and
put the acid on (someone): to ask someone for a loan: the ultimate test of genuine friendship — from the acid test by which the genuineness of gold is tested, as gold is unaffected by nitric acid.

Some World War I slang has disappeared, simply because modern circumstances no longer need such expressions:

Anzac stew: an urn of hot water and one bacon rind; made famous by Lieutenant General Birdwood ('Birdie'), the Anzac commander at Gallipoli;

Anzac wafer: a very hard biscuit; and

Anzac soup: water in a shell-hole polluted by a corpse.

Other slang expressions from the same time and circumstances have also disappeared, although they remain perfectly serviceable:

chivoo: a party or celebration (from the French *chez vous:* at your place);

catsow: the price of a beer — twopence (from the French *quatre sous*);

jildy: quickly (*on the jildy* — in a hurry) from Hindi;

kangaroo feathers: a furphy; an impossible thing;

kennel-up: stop talking; and

macnoon: mad or dippy (from the colloquial Egyptian Arabic *magnoon* — mad).

The exigencies of trench warfare made it likely that an expression would emerge to describe the ground between your own trenches and the enemy's: *no man's land*. It is an expression in common use today, with a weaker meaning for weaker circumstances.

No man's land has a much longer history than its current use suggests. From the ninth century to about the eighteenth century, *no man* (or *noman*) was a common synonym for *no-one* or *nobody*. In recorded use from the early fourteenth century, *no man's land* simply meant land belonging to nobody. For centuries, *no man's land* was unoccupied and benign (at best), or waste land, dark with foreboding (at worst). However in a country that was relatively densely populated, unowned land was likely to have some fundamental defect. For that reason, perhaps, the expression *no man's land* acquired a negative connotation. The *OED2* gives a quotation (in Latin) from 1326 which has the unfortunate Arnold taken to *nonesmanneslond* outside London, where he was beheaded. But in 1881, Thomas Hughes (author of *Tom Brown's School Days*) writes of a 'small plot of nomans land in the woods'.

In World War I, *no man's land* was the stretch of disputed ground for which a terrible price was paid. Paradoxically, the price paid would render the real estate worthless, except to generals. In this modern world of more remote, impersonal killing techniques, no mans's land has reverted to its earlier sense.

STRANGE BEGINNINGS

———◆———

The 23 April 1884 issue of the *Trade Marks Journal* included a note that Burroughs, Wellcome & Company, Snow Hill Buildings, Holborn Viaduct, London, E.C. had been registered as proprietor of the trade name *Tabloid* for use in connection with pharmaceutical products. The word was an invented one, derived from *tablet*, with the familiar *-oid* suffix. It was used to describe and label tablets that were relatively small and contained a concentrated dose of the relevant drug.

The new format was popular, and the word quickly came to be understood outside its field of origin. It also came to be used by others, at which point Burroughs Wellcome sued. The Court of Appeal held that the word had acquired a secondary meaning outside pharmacology. Byrne J said:

> The word *Tabloid* has become so well-known in consequence of the use of it by the Plaintiff firm in

connection with their compressed drugs that I think it has acquired a secondary sense in which it has been used and may legitimately be used so long as it does not interfere with their trade rights. I think the word has been so applied generally with reference to the notion of a compressed form or dose of anything.' (see *re Burroughs Wellcome & Co's Trade Mark*, (1904) 21 RPC 217)).

Meanwhile, in 1894, the Harmsworth brothers (Alfred and Harold, later Lord Northcliffe and Lord Rothermere respectively) bought a failing newspaper, the *London Evening News*, and revised its contents by ensuring that news items were short and easily digested. They then established the *Daily Mail*, which was first published on 4 May 1896. It was advertised as 'The penny newspaper for one halfpenny' and 'The busy man's daily journal'. Its style was short and to the point. What it lacked in depth, it made up in brevity. It became very successful. The style of newspaper pioneered by the Harmsworth brothers was quite soon referred to as 'tabloid news'.

Tabloid has no current use other than in connection with this style of journalism. It is used to describe the format of a newspaper, as well as the style of journalism generally found in those newspapers. It is also used to describe television and radio journalism that is superficial or sensational. Strangely, its true signification today is the opposite of what was originally intended, since the news dosage in tabloid journalism is not only not concentrated, but diluted to almost homeopathic levels. I imagine that, if the word were used today to refer to a medicine, people would think it an odd misuse of the word.

By a curious symmetry, Alfred Harmsworth's first venture into journalism was a small gossip sheet which carried innocuous items of social news. It was called *Tit-Bits*. He probably did not realise just how close he had come to the late-twentieth century meaning of tabloid journalism.

Among other consciously invented words, *serendipity* has also lodged firmly in our language. The Arab name for the island now called Sri Lanka was *Serendib*, apparently a corruption of the Sanskrit *Simhaladvipa* ('Dwelling-Place-of-Lions Island'). Horace Walpole was much impressed by a story about three princes who lived on the island, and whose adventures were largely guided by luck. It was called 'The Three Princes of Serendip'. He coined the expression *serendipity* as a noun for the idea of lucky accident and chance discovery. Although the word was not much used for 150 years, it was rediscovered in the early twentieth century, and is now in common use.

It took 150 years for *serendipity* to find its place in the sun, which illustrates what haphazard forces shape our language. It serves almost the same function as *haphazard*, which has a much longer history. Strictly, *haphazard* is an example of pleonasm: the two elements of the word have the same meaning. *Hap* is a Middle English word meaning 'chance or luck'. It does not survive on its own, but is found in compounds such as *mishap* and *happenstance*, and (in an altered sense) in *happen*.

For centuries, Arab women used powdered antimony to

colour their eyelids. The powder was called *al kohl*, and was produced by a process of sublimation, the process of vaporising a compound solid then condensing the vapour to precipitate the desired powder. Many substances can be produced by sublimation, but when Western alchemists discovered the process of sublimation, they used an anglicised form of the Arab *al kohl* to describe the result: hence, *alcohol of sulphur*, for sulphur powder produced by sublimation; and *alcohol martis*, for reduced iron. By extension, *alcohol* came to mean the essence of a thing, or the product of sublimation or distillation. During the eighteenth century, it came to refer principally to rectified spirits produced by distillation. Although *kohl* is still understood in its original sense as powder for colouring eyelids, *alcohol* has moved on.

Petard is a curious word for several reasons: it is almost exclusively used in the context of a single quotation; and its meaning is not generally known. (This second feature may not much distinguish it). The quotation in which it is best known, and most often used, is from Shakespeare (*Hamlet* Act 3 scene iv): 'For 'tis the sport to have the enginer hoist on his own petard'.

A *petard* was a box that was filled with gunpowder and placed against a door or wall. When the charge was ignited, the charge would generally blow a hole in the adjacent surface. (Later, limpet mines would do a similar job.) However, it was an unreliable device, and it often happened that the device fired prematurely, or with unpredicted force. The engineer who was arming the petard would thus be blown into the air ('hoist'), causing merriment among the uncaring. (Nowadays, witnesses to such an event would receive grief counselling and compensation; and playwrights would not dare make light of it). Engineers were not so well regarded in Shakespeare's time. Nor, it seems, was the device itself. *Petard* is a French word. It means *a fart*.

Of course, it is not unusual for impolite words to creep unnoticed into polite speech. If we forget their origins, we can easily miss their sting. Few people would hesitate before using such words as *bumf, snafu, berk*, and *poppycock*.

Bumf is short for bum-fodder; *berk* is rhyming slang for *Berkshire hunt* (scil. *cunt*); *snafu* is an acronym for *Situation Normal: All Fucked Up*; *poppycock* comes from the Dutch *pappekak*, literally 'soft shit'. Unless your companions know the true meaning of these words, you can use them in the most polite society and get away scot-free.

Calendar is another word with an interesting history — and the idea it currently signifies has an equally interesting history. Until 46 BC, the Roman year was divided into lunar months: that is, months of 28 days. In that year, Julius Caesar sought advice from an astronomer, Sosigenes, about reform of the calendar. Sosigenes advised Caesar to abandon the lunar calendar in favour of a solar one, recognising a year of 365 days. (The accuracy of astronomical observations in pre-Christian times is startling, considering the difficulties later encountered by Galileo and others when they advocated the Copernican view of the world.)

The Romans recognised three important days in each month. The middle day of each month was named the *idus* (the word is the root of *divide*). The ninth day before the *iudes* was the *nones*. The first day was the *kalends*.

The *iudes* of a month is familiar to us as the *ides*: specifically the *ides of March*, of which Julius Caesar was warned (see *Julius Caesar* I ii 17); but each month had its *ides*. When the Roman calendar was reformed in 46 BC, two months were added and the number of days in each month was adjusted, to bring the cycle of months into closer agreement with the equinoxes. As a result, the ides of a month became either the 13th or the 15th.

The first day of each month was the *kalends*. The *kalends* was an important day because, on that day, by convention, bills were due for payment. Not surprisingly, merchants would compile lists of accounts due for payment on the kalends of a given month, and the list was called a *calendarium*.

In Old French, *calendier* meant a list or register. In English, it retains that sense. Thus we have the Court calendar, the calendar of Saints, the calendar of prisoners at the assizes, and so on. This meaning is subordinated to the primary meaning — namely, the system according to which the year is divided into months and days and, by extension, a document recording that division for one or more years.

STRANGE PLURALS

———◆———

Some words take a plural form, but never the corresponding singular form. This, despite the fact that the singular form of the thing signified is clearly imaginable.

So, we refer to *pants,* or a *pair of pants*; to *trousers* or a *pair of trousers*; to *scissors* or a *pair of scissors*; to *tweezers* or a *pair of tweezers.* Each of the things signified can exist as a singular, and each of the words is a true English plural word. But we never refer to a *pant* (except in the fashion industry) or a *trouser* or a *scissor.* It might be permissible to speak of a *tweezer,* but it does not sound right.

When a pair of scissors is separated into its two parts for sharpening, we do not have *two scissors;* instead, we have two objects which have no obvious name. When a one-legged person has his trousers specially made, does he buy a *trouser* or *half a pair of trousers*?

We refer to *clothes,* meaning several items of clothing. It is obviously a useful and common expression for useful and common things. But just as several items of clothing are useful and common, so is the single item. However, when we wish to speak of a single item of clothing, it is necessary either to identify it by type ('pick up that pullover; try on that skirt') or else refer to it cumbersomely as 'that item of clothing'.

English has a prodigious vocabulary, with words to describe the rarest things and the most obscure ideas. It gives us *ulotrichous* ('a member of the race of people characterised by crisp or woolly hair'); and *sciolist* ('a false pretender to knowledge': a word I heard first in 1964, and have never heard or read since). It also offers *syzygy* (a word I have never had occasion to use apart from this essay), definitions of which include:

> *Math.* A group of rational integral functions so related that, on their being severally multiplied by other rational integral functions, the sum of the products vanishes identically; also, the relation between such functions).

It is a mystery that English lacks (or avoids) such obvious and useful words as a *trouser* or a *scissor* or a *clothe*.

Shibboleth is a word that is often misused, although in its proper English meaning it is useful. It is sometimes used now as meaning a 'myth' or 'misapprehension'. Funk (*Thereby Hangs a Tale*, p. 256) goes so far as to say that it means any catch-cry or slogan used by a political party. Except on the Humpty Dumpty principle, this is wrong.

It was introduced into English in Wyclif's *Bible*, and its extensive entry in *OED2* includes the following usages:

1. The Hebrew word used by Jephthah as a test-word by which to distinguish the fleeing Ephraimites (who could not pronounce the *sh*) from his own men the Gileadites (Judges xii. 4–6).

1382 Wyclif Judges xii. 6 Thei askiden hym, Seye thanne Sebolech [**1535** Coverdale Schiboleth, **1611** Shibboleth]

2. transf.

a. A word or sound which a person is unable to pronounce correctly; a word used as a test for detecting foreigners, or persons from another district, by their pronunciation.

1827 Scott *Two Drovers* i, In attempting to teach his companion to utter, with true precision, the shibboleth Llhu, which is the Gaelic for a calf.

b. A peculiarity of pronunciation or accent indicative of a person's origin.

c. loosely. A custom, habit, mode of dress, or the like, which distinguishes a particular class or set of persons.

1806 A. Hunter Culina (ed. 2) 192 Custard and apple-pie is the Shibboleth by which an Alderman may be known.

3. fig. A catchword or formula adopted by a party or sect, by which their adherents or followers may be discerned, or those not their followers may be excluded.

b. The mode of speech distinctive of a profession, class, etc.

1849 Macaulay *Hist. Eng.* iii. I. 400 To that sanctimonious jargon, which was his shibboleth, was opposed another jargon not less absurd.

So the true meaning of *shibboleth* is a secret test word or unconscious social discriminator.

It also has a characteristic as a word in the English language which is, so far as I am aware, unique. This is not the fact that it is a Hebrew word borrowed into English: the *OED2* gives over 400 of them. It is that its adopted meaning, from the very outset, bears no connection with its meaning in the language from which it is borrowed. In Hebrew it was 'an ear of corn' or 'a stream in flood'.

We borrowed it, not for what it meant, but for the way it was used: to detect a mispronunciation.

❦

The English language displays all its quirkiness in the matter of plurals. The oddities are often disguised, because English is a relatively uninflected language, and mismatches of number can easily pass unnoticed. So, in the sentence 'What odds do you suggest?', there is no way of knowing — thus no need to decide — whether *odds* is a singular or plural noun. The *s* at the end is not necessarily a reliable guide, as I will show.

The hearty smorgasbord of English offers such delicacies as words that are plural in form but treated as singular; and words which are singular in form but treated as plural. There are plurals that refuse to admit of a singular; and singular words that do not admit of a plural.

For example *physics, mathematics, economics, linguistics,* and *hydraulics* are all words that are singular in sense and are construed as singular, despite their form. They do not have plurals. *Politics,* and *ethics,* by contrast, are construed as plural but do not readily admit a singular form. *Arithmetic* and *logic* are singular in sense and form, but do not readily accept a plural.

Acoustics and *aesthetics* remain ambivalent: they look and act like plurals, but among the hard-edged chic they are also used in the singular: *The Playhouse has a very dry acoustic/pre-modern aesthetic.* Apart from the fashion statement implicit in the choice of form, however, the idea conveyed remains unchanged: the singular and the plural mean the same thing.

Pants, trousers, breeches, scissors, shears, bellows, spectacles, and *glasses* are all plural in form, and they need a plural verb: *These trousers are too small; these scissors are blunt.* The curiosity is that we often re-double the plural character of the things by referring to *a pair of* pants, scissors, etc. Yet the semantically identical *two scissors, two bellows* would be absurd.

In the fashion industry, where the quest for variety is ceaseless, it is common now to hear references to *a nice pant* or *a smart trouser.* But although the gurus of fashion often treat us to a *spectacle*, they do not use the word in reference to eyewear. Perhaps that too will come, when the monocle reclaims its place as a fashion accessory.

By contrast, *news, mews,* and *molasses* are plural in form but take the singular, whether the particular instance of the thing is one or many.

So, 'the news is bad', whether the news under discussion is a single item or the entire contents of a newspaper. It was not always so: even during the reign of Queen Victoria, it was common to say 'the news are bad'. In modern French *les nouvelles de l'Angleterre sont mauvaises* still.

Mews was originally plural: *mewing* is a synonym for *moulting*; and a *mew* was a cage for a mewing hawk. The mews were moved to make way for the king's stables; and the stables were later moved to make way for fashionable and expensive housing. As the stables gave way to desirable accommodation, the unequivocal plural became a collective singular: *a mews*.

Molasses derives ultimately from the Latin root for honey: *mell-*. It was introduced into English from the French *melasse*, but was originally introduced in the plural form as *melasus*. The fact that it is treated as singular is understandable: like many nouns of multitude, the emphasis is on the undifferentiated bulk rather than a specific portion. But the gratuitous use of the plural form is unaccountable.

What the lawyers call *fungibles* are often nouns of multitude: *wheat, barley, rice*, etc. Each is singular. To distinguish the individual example from the aggregate, it is necessary to refer to *a grain of wheat, an ear of corn*, etc. An exception to this pattern is *oats*, which is an orthodox plural of *oat*, although the singular form is rarely used. One grain of oats is just *an oat*. Compounding this curiosity, *porridge* has for a long time been regarded in English and Scottish as a collective plural: *These porridge are too cold* is correct, and in Scotland it is current; but (in Australia at least) it is rare.

Other nouns of multitude, such as *public, parliament, government, company*, etc can be treated as singular or plural, depending on whether the emphasis is on the collection or the individuals constituting it. *The government are considering changing the regulations* suggests that individuals within the government are doing the considering. This usage has an outdated air to it, perhaps because our system of government puts little store on individual thought among its members.

To add to the confusion, *parliament, government*, and *company* can take a plural form, but the meaning conveyed is quite different.

Assets was originally construed as a singular word despite its form, because it was used adjectivally. It began life as the Latin *ad satis*: to sufficiency, and is reflected in the modern French *assez*: enough. In Law French, *aver assets* meant 'to have enough' (that is, enough to satisfy a judgement or demand). In particular, it meant *Goods enough to discharge that burthen, which is cast upon the executor or heir, in satisfying the testator's or ancestor's debts and legacies*. Soon enough, the form of the word led to its being treated as a noun and construed as a plural, and it lost the connotation of sufficiency. To complain that you do not have enough assets would once have been nonsensical — indeed self-contradictory — but is now a common complaint, and well understood.

Although *assets* readily admits the singular *asset*, the corresponding *goods* will not. 'She had not a good or chattel to her name' is a familiar idea, but uncomfortable English. Why *goods* should not readily admit of the singular form is a mystery. In a different meaning, *good* can be used in the singular: 'this is all to the good'. But it remains intractably plural in its commonest usage.

Some of the strangest contradictions are seen in the heartland of plurality: numbers. *One head of cattle; two dozen head of cattle; three hundred head of cattle; four hundred thousand head of cattle* … All these constructions are perfectly good English. Likewise, it is usual to say that a country has *a population of 18 million*. Why not *two hundreds, two hundred thousands, 18 millions*? It seems that we readily treat numerals as collective nouns, although it is difficult to see any unifying principle to determine when this should be done.

By contrast, we readily speak of people arriving in *ones and twos*, or being at *sixes and sevens*, or meeting for *elevenses*. These are all idiomatic. But when a plural form is logically suggested, we cling to the singular. The most striking exception to this is the idiomatic expression *on all fours. On all four* would make perfect sense, but rendering *four* in the plural is inexplicable.

Most collective nouns retain their form whether they are treated as singular or plural: *the public* are *dissatisfied with the taxation system; the public* is *disturbed by the increase in crime*. By contrast, some numbers readily take a plural form but are treated as collective plurals: *Many thousands of people were seen at the rally/Ten thousand people were seen at the rally*.

And while we are speaking of people, we lawyers have a strange ambivalence about the plural of *person*. In ordinary conversation we speak of *one person* and *many people*. But give us a document to draft or a judge to address, and it is *one person* and *many persons*. In the same way, we refer conversationally, with no risk of misunderstanding, to a person withdrawing all her *money* from the bank. But in court, she deals with all her *monies*. It is a curious thing that the formality of legal proceedings induces us to lapse into irregular plurals.

Few would recognise *stamina* and *truce* as plurals, or *peas* and *cherries* as singular. Once it was so. The *stamen* is a thread-like structure in plants. It was also one of the threads spun for our lives by the Fates, in Roman mythology. These threads were thought to be responsible for our individual vitality. The plural of *stamen* is *stamina*.

Trewe/triewe was a Middle English word which meant 'truth or fidelity to a promise, good faith, assurance of faith, promise'. It was generally used in the plural, and spelled variously as *triews, trwys, trues*, etc until the spelling *truce* emerged in the sixteenth century and stabilised in the eighteenth century. Thus, *truce* is a plural.

What we now call *peas* are botanically *pisum sativum*. The word entered English as *pease* (singular), but was commonly supposed to be plural because of its form, and because it is generally used as a collective noun. By backformation, *pea* emerged as the singular. In a similar way, the cherry entered English at the time of the Norman conquest as *cyrs* or *ciris*, from the French *cerise*, which is still used in English as a colour. That old-fashioned girl, Eartha Kitt, wanted 'an old-fashioned car, a cerise Cadillac — long enough to fit a bowling-alley in the back'.

The form of *ciris* drifted long before Eartha Kitt ordered her Cadillac; in the seventeenth century it was *cheryse*.

Sounding plural, it was treated as plural, and the singular forms *cherie*, *cherrie* and, finally, *cherry* emerged.

Means, in the sense of *method*, is sensibly understood as a singular notion, but only takes the plural: *The means he used were deplorable*. In the same way, *thanks* may refer to a single expression of gratitude, but only allows the plural form: *His thanks were gratefully received*. Neither *means* nor *thanks* has a singular form. *Alms, amends, bounds, confines, grounds, aerobics,* and *hustings* all have the same characteristics. By contrast, *innings* in cricket can be either singular or plural, depending on the intention of the speaker.

In a different way, *odds* will be either singular or plural, depending on the sense intended by the speaker. *Odds* means the difference between several things, the condition of being unequal, or disparity in number. It is commonly encountered in the colloquial expression *to be at odds with someone* — that is, to be in a position different to that of the other person. In this sense, it is singular despite its form. Another colloquialism preserves a hint of the singular: *What's the odds?* means *What is the difference?* It is otherwise for the *odds* in gaming, which is plural. It has no singular: even a single wager has plural odds.

Data and *media* are two words increasingly used by journalists and others as singulars. They are convenient in the singular; and well understood. This is currently causing irritation and anxiety among the learned, because they are unquestionably plural. The battle rages quietly in clubs and correspondence columns. But let me offer a word of advice to the learned: look at all the words discussed above, and give up the fight.

TERMINAL PREPOSITIONS

—————◆—————

English grammar, like English history, is scattered with myths, the origins of which we can only guess at. One, as we have seen, is that infinitives must not be split. Perhaps times are changing for that one: there seems now to be a tendency to boldly split infinitives that have never been split before.

Another is that a sentence should not end with a preposition. This idea has three remarkable features. First, the ardour with which it is embraced has built progressively over the centuries, while many other aspects of proper grammar have fallen into disuse. Second, even into the twenty-first century it continues to be repeated and insisted on. And third, the desperate need to avoid a terminal preposition drives otherwise rational people into grammatical contortions of the most grotesque sort.

The word *preposition* comes from the Latin *praeposition-em* which is self-explanatory: it seems to insist that the thing be put *before* the noun or pronoun it governs. In the *Oxford*

Companion to English, Tom McArthur explains that, because of the original meaning of *preposition*, 'the classical prescriptive rule emerged for standard English that sentences should not end with a preposition.' Nevertheless, in early times of innocence, even writers of the first rank ended sentences with prepositions, leaving the relative far behind. Shakespeare was a frequent offender:

> Now all the blessings Of a glad father, compasse thee about. (*The Tempest* v. i. 180)
>
> The day is broke, be wary, looke about. (*Romeo and Juliet* iii. v. 40)
>
> And let me speake to th' yet unknowing world How these things came about. (*Hamlet* v. ii. 391)
>
> Indeede I am in the waste two yards about. (*Merry Wives of Windsor* i. ii. 44)
>
> We have some secrets to confer about. (*Two Gentlemen of Verona* iii. i. 2)

He was not alone:

> A great altar to see to. (*Bible* Joshua 22:10)
>
> They are the fittest timber to make great politiques of. (Bacon *Of Goodness* and *Goodness of Nature)*
>
> Let us descend and see if we can meet with more honor and honesty in the next world we shall touch upon. (Aphra Behn *Oroonoko* or *The Royal Slave*)
>
> The subject was too delicate to question Johnson upon. (Boswell *Life of Dr Johnson*)

'Yes,' said the good lady, who now knew what ground we were
upon. (Charlotte Bronte *Jane Eyre*)

When the Fowler brothers published *The King's English*
in 1906, they inadvertently gave offence with its opening
sentence. Longer than is now fashionable, other than in the
law reports, it occupies an entire paragraph. It reads:

> The compilers of this book would be wanting in courtesy
> if they did not expressly say what might otherwise be
> safely left to the reader's discernment: the frequent
> appearances in it of any author's or newspaper's name
> does not mean that that author or newspaper offends
> more often than others against rules of grammar or style;
> it merely shows that they have been among the necessarily
> limited number chosen to collect instances from.

A reviewer dismissed the book out of hand on account of
that sentence. But the Fowler brothers had not intended to be
provocative. The matter was of no account to them: *The King's
English* contains no discussion of terminal prepositions. As
H.W. Fowler remarked in a note to the 1930 edition: 'it had
not occurred to us to examine seriously the validity of what,
superstition or no, is a widespread belief.'

The sentence irritated a lot of people who, as irritated
people tend to do, wrote corrective letters. H.W. Fowler got
his quiet revenge in *Modern English Usage* (1927), with an
entry under the topic: 'Preposition at End'. Having ignored
the subject in 1906, Fowler amasses, in just two pages,

overwhelming evidence to demonstrate that the anxiety which afflicts so many English speakers is nothing but a 'cherished superstition'. He marshals dozens of examples of final prepositions in work by the great writers of English. Burchfield, in his third edition of *Modern English Usage*, describes the phenomenon as 'one of the most persistent myths about prepositions'.

Fowler's research suggests that the original culprit was Dryden, who 'went through all his prefaces contriving away all the final prepositions he had been guilty of in his first editions'. (It is lucky for us all that Dryden wrote after Shakespeare, or we might have lost the reassurance Shakespeare offers by his frequent excursions into the forbidden territory). Dryden's zeal left its mark on generations of school children. Even now, when most people are taught very little grammar, most seem to know the 'rule' about final prepositions. The matter is made the more absurd (and difficult) because some words are both prepositions and adverbs, in which case the dictates of usage and folklore are different according to the role played. Examples of prepositions which can also be adverbs are: *about, beside, beyond, forth, inward, midway, near, off, round, round about*, and *since*.

Despite the tenacity of the superstition, it remains true that style is the determining consideration. Some sentences would be absurd with the preposition at the end; others may be constructed with the preposition at the end or not, according to taste; others again will be unreasonably distorted if the imagined rule is allowed to intimidate good sense.

In the following examples, the alternatives do not work, even as a joke:

She went into the church.
The church is what she went into.

I look forward to meeting you.
Meeting you is what I look forward to.

In the following, the choice is one of taste: more formal or less?

I wanted a seat from which I could see the game.
I wanted a seat I could see the game from.

For which firm do you work?
Which firm do you work for?

In some sentences, only recasting will remove the supposed problem:

The bed had not been slept in.
No-one had slept in the bed.

What did you do that for?
Why did you do that?

At the end of his entry about final prepositions, Fowler offers the following advice:

Follow no arbitrary rule, but remember that there are often two or more possible arrangements between which a choice should be consciously made; if the abnormal, or at least unorthodox, final preposition that has naturally presented itself sounds comfortable, keep it; if it does not sound comfortable, still keep it if it has compensating vigour, or when among awkward possibilities it is the least awkward.

It was some years later that a departmental memo, which had gone to extreme lengths to avoid a final preposition, drove Churchill to note in the margin: 'This is the sort of English up with which I will not put'. It is a sentiment most would agree with.

The durable myth that educated people should not end a sentence with a preposition was neatly exploited by a Chicago reporter in the aftermath of the Loeb-Leopold trial (1924). After 12 years in prison, Dickie Loeb was stabbed to death by another prisoner, James Day. Day was charged with his murder. His defence was that Loeb had made a homosexual advance, and that he was defending himself. With more wit than taste, the journalist wrote: 'Richard Loeb, despite his erudition, ended his sentence with a proposition.'

VESTIGIAL REMAINS

———————◆———————

Our language is sprinkled with the vestigial remains of words whose original use has been lost, overtaken, or abandoned. Clues can be found in some compound words — words made up by linking two other words. In many instances, the elements of the compound maintain a sturdy independent existence: *liftwell, businessman, housewife, bookcase.*

In others, however, only one of the elements survives independently. Take *quagmire*, for example. A *mire* is a piece of wet, swampy ground, a boggy place in which one may be engulfed or stick fast. A *quag* is a marshy or boggy spot, especially one covered with turf, which shakes or yields when walked on.

Quagmire once had a number of variants: *quamire, quakemire, qualemire,* and *quavemire. Quake* is well known independently as a verb, and in *earthquake*, but its compound with *mire* is obsolete. *Quave* ('to quake, shake or tremble') has disappeared, but its cognate *quaver* survives. Another cognate, *quaverous,* ('tremulous, quavering') sounds well and suggests its own meaning, but has lost the battle to *tremulous*. *Quag*, although reported by *OED2* as used in 1904, seems to be well along the path to extinction.

A curious aspect of *quagmire* is why it emerged in the first place. *Quag* and *mire* seem to be pretty near synonyms, except perhaps to serious bog fanciers. What greater intensity does a tract of boggy country get from teaming *quag* with *mire*? And why then does the onomatopoeic *quag* disappear while *mire* survives?

In a similar state of decline is *monger* ('a dealer, trader or trafficker'). It formed part of many mercantile compounds: *cheesemonger, ironmonger, costermonger, fishmonger*, and so on. I can remember these words being in ordinary use. But in the past 30 years or so in Australia, they have taken on an outmoded air. Perhaps this has happened as the specialised traders they describe have diversified their activities, or been absorbed in larger enterprises. So the cheesemonger's trade has been absorbed by the delicatessen; the ironmonger's by the hardware store; the costermonger (originally meaning 'apple seller') by the greengrocer or fruiterer; and all of them by the supermarket.

There are two curious features about this linguistic fade-out. First, in most cases the replacement word describes the shop where the trade is carried on, whereas the original - *monger* compounds described the trader himself. Second, there does remain a need for such words (as awkward constructions such as *fruiterer* attest). Despite the supermarket mentality of our age, specialist shops exist which sell only fruit, or fish, or cheese. At any good market there are people who trade only in a narrow range of goods. But although the London barrow-man, who sells fruit and vegetables, still calls himself a *costermonger*, the man who supplies apples (and nothing else) to the market does not. (*Costerd* and *custard* both mean apple: the so-called *custard-apple* is a pleonasm).

Some shop names refer to the trader, not the trade. One example is *grocer*. It is from the old French *grossier*: a person who bought 'in gross' or in bulk. Its meaning has narrowed. Another example is the *butcher*. Its current use has widened from its original meaning. A butcher is one who slaughters and sells meat. Strictly, he does more than the fleshmonger, but the shop still carries the (inaccurate) name of the trader who used to slaughter the animal before selling its meat. The butcher originally specialised in goat's meat: the word comes from the French *bouc*, from which we get *buck*: a he-goat. It is probably a very long time since a true butcher carried on business in an Australian shopping centre.

Nowadays, *monger* survives primarily in disparaging compounds such as *scandalmonger* and *rumourmonger*. It also survives, although not in common use, in *fleshmonger*, meaning a fornicator or pander. Perhaps the butcher is wise to misdescribe himself.

Index of Main Words

Index of Main Words